Hope Pay The Wages

How To Deal With The Personal Impact Of A Struggling Business

ANDREW R MILLER

Copyright © 2012 Andrew R Miller

All rights reserved. No part of this book may be reproduced in any material form (including photocopying or storing in any medium by electronic means) without written permission of the copyright owners.

ISBN: 1480042382
ISBN-13: 978- 1480042384

Put all of your efforts into everything you do,

but not all your hopes.

TESTIMONIALS FOR THE AUTHOR

The word 'Coaching' is getting used for so many things these days that it is fantastic to see and hear a coach who definitely knows their stuff - and with my background in corporate L&D I have come across many so-called 'Coaches' in my time. Over recent months, I have faced a number of challenging situations on a personal level, that have arisen as a result of a company I was working for going into administration and leaving me with some fantastic opportunities to choose from, but not really knowing which way to turn.

Andrew demonstrated his knowledge of the insolvency process and it was clear from his warmth and approach that he had an appreciation for how and why I was feeling the way I was. In a true coaching style - Andrew never once told me the answer, he just listened on all levels, (he was able to sense the emotion behind it) and then questioned me about what I wanted and where I wanted to go. At the end of the coaching with Andrew, not only had he made me feel like a huge weight had been lifted from my shoulders, I had been able to draw my own conclusion about the direction I should go in. Not once did Andrew pass comment or judgement - he just used his friendly, approachable style and his knowledge of business to enable ME to see where I wanted to go.

I would have no hesitation in personally recommending Andrew - if you're struggling, if your company is about to or did go into Administration then you can't stay with the past forever, at some point you need to move on and sometimes a little help to guide us there is all you will need.
Linda Ladley, Bridging the Gap 2 Ltd

I like the fact that Andrew has recognised that there are the mechanics of business support and advice and stuff like that, but there actually isn't anything for the individuals involved: as people; as human beings that worry and think about "what's the worst that could happen?"
Haworth Ward-Drummond, Estate Planner

Andrew spent an afternoon coaching myself and my management team. He left us feeling positive, energetic, as if we could take on the world! Andrew is one of the most positive people I've ever met and his knowledge is immense.
Caroline Andrew-Johnstone, Fas-Print

Meeting Andrew has been a humbling experience and a real pleasure. He has been a real inspiration and his guidance is much appreciated.

Right from the beginning Andrew pushed me to look at my personal values and career interests from different angles and analyse them within various parameters, thereby forcing me to analyse my strengths/weaknesses and interests in great detail.

Working with Andrew has been a great learning curve and a valuable experience, which I will always cherish, and hope to be able to pass on to someone else in due course.

Pardeep Jakhar, Chartered Accountant

Andrew's personality is one of his greatest assets. Andrew definitely "walks his walk" and "talks his talk" and is a credit to the profession. I doubt I would have been able to run my own business so smoothly and confidently had it not been for Andrew's support.

Claire Turnbull, Recruitment Consultant and Coach

I was concerned about some of the issues that might crop up, however, Andrew has really helped. I feel lighter and there is a strange calming feeling. I'm now looking at things from a positive angle.

It feels like someone's stuck a vacuum cleaner into my brain and sucked out all the sh*t, like a good spring clean.

This session has made me realise that I can achieve what I want. The possibility is there. I feel positive about my future for the first time in many years.

Jennifer Gleeson, Hotel General Manager

CONTENTS

	Acknowledgements	i
	Foreword by Andrew Cawkwell, TMA (UK)	ii
	Preface	iv
	Introduction	vi
	How to Read this Book	xii
	Caveat	xiv
1	Two Types of Stress	1
2	The Slippery Slope	22
3	The Inaction Trap	38
4	There is Always a Choice	50
5	Dealing with the Bank	72
6	The Biggest Problem	107
7	Fear is the Mindkiller	126
8	The Traditional Label of Failure	144
9	Getting Back On The Horse	163
10	What Am I Going To Do Next?	174
11	Summary and Conclusions	208
	Afterword	224
	Glossary	226
	About the Author	242

ACKNOWLEDGEMENTS

A big thank you to the following people.

Gail Powell, without whom I would not have written this book as quickly as I did.

Dr. John Lockhart, for proof-reading the final document.

To Sharon, for her support throughout the process.

And, of course, thank you to all of the contributors for revealing their innermost secrets. You know who you are.

FOREWORD

As a board director of the Turnaround Management Association (UK) and a partner of Newtons Solicitors Limited, I work directly with directors facing financial difficulties and am in constant contact with other professionals looking to help them.

I met Andrew a couple of years ago when he was just starting out on his new venture, before this book had even been contemplated. I instantly recognised the relevance of what he was trying to achieve and that he had identified an area of the turnaround industry where support is virtually non-existent. The personal element.

Now, having read this book, I believe that Andrew has produced something that is unique, highly significant and essential reading for anyone that is or has been involved in the management of a business which is stressed or distressed.

I am also in no doubt that anyone advising such businesses (including Insolvency Practitioners, Turnaround Practitioners, Accountants and Bankers) will benefit enormously, both through reading it themselves and through introducing it to their clients.

"Hope Won't Pay the Wages" clearly and succinctly explains the experiences and stresses which company directors face when going through the life cycle of a business in a way which I have never seen before in the marketplace.

So often there will be situations where a director of a company needs answers, which may seem like very basic questions to those involved in the industry. The director may not know who to ask or where to turn to for answers. What this book does incredibly well is to draw together experiences from directors who have gone through an insolvency and put them across in a way which makes it easy to understand.

It is also a book which all advisors should read as it will help them understand first hand the pain that directors go through when contemplating placing a business into insolvency and properly enable them to empathise with the situation. This will allow them to give a much greater level of support to their clients.

"Hope Won't Pay the Wages" is a 'must have' read and is something that I will certainly be recommending to my clients and colleagues within the TMA.

Andrew Cawkwell
Board Director of TMA (UK)
Newtons Solicitors Limited

PREFACE

In my previous line of work, I was involved with a lot of companies that had gone bust. Consequently, I knew a lot of directors and business owners that had suffered the mental torture of watching their enterprise, that they had spent so long building up, collapse before their eyes.

Once the dust has settled and they are back on their feet again, every single person says the same thing.

> *"It was one of the worst periods of my life...but I learnt so much as a result."*

As someone whose business is based on helping people, the natural next step was to find out precisely what they had learnt and to pass those lessons on.

So, I started talking to as many people as I could that had been through a corporate insolvency.

I spoke to a wide range of directors, both men and women, and covered many types of business. From large international exporters to coastal town souvenir shops. From manufacturing enterprises to service industries.

Naturally, there were many issues specific to individual situations but, quite quickly, some common themes started to emerge.

This book provides you with the key themes and learning points arising from those interviews.

Every quote that you see in this book is a genuine quote from one of the people that I interviewed. I have tried to recreate them as accurately as possible, including the grammar, phrasing and hesitations that they used. Where editing was necessary, I have ensured that the spirit of the comment remains.

I have not identified the individuals concerned as the interviews were carried out confidentially. This was at my insistence, not theirs, as every tale involves other people and companies and it is not right that they be prejudiced by anything written here.

I can tell you, however, that every person I spoke to was an ordinary, honest, hard working, well meaning individual. Victims of circumstance, rather than having done anything particularly wrong.

And every one of them went through hell.

Make sure that you don't.

INTRODUCTION

> *"It's just too agonising. Too much heartache. It's too much heartache to go through. All that pressure. There was nobody to go to ... to help you. There was just YOU!"*

"The mental and emotional things of ... being in business for yourself and wanting something to work. And kind of knowing at the back of your mind that it isn't happening but still trying to push through and put a brave face on it."

> *"And I remember ... I don't know whether it was depression or not ... but feeling really really low. When I'd go through this cycle of 'I can't do this'. I used to hate ... absolutely despise it. Sunday night ... couldn't sleep because I didn't want to go into work. Even at work I'd do anything I could to avoid talking to customers and ... I remember ... sitting there behind my desk one day and ... er ... I don't think I was in tears but being close to tears thinking 'I hate this, I hate this, I hate this!'"*

"It was one of the most difficult times in my life really. When you look back, you forget. I see it with people I meet now. See it with people struggling. I could have done with somebody to show me the way through."

> *"I felt really scared. Really, really, really scared.*

Of failure. For a really long time. I was petrified. And that ... that actually came out in my home life as well. It transgressed from work to my home life and it did that for a long time. For many, many years."

"There was a lot of confusion back then. Failing business. A failing business that I didn't want to work. No heart in it. Considering going back to my old job - or ... what else? It was just this confusion. It was horrible, I just hated it. It was just a lonely time."

"It was pure hell leading up to it. Because of the pressure of the debt that the company had got itself into and then having to make the decision. It was realising the depth that the company'd got itself into and then having to say 'Well, what are we going to do?' It was the darkest hour to say 'Well, we're going to put it into liquidation.' That was the darkest hour. It's all the emotional stuff. It's that, that kills you."

"I didn't have anything. All their venom was directed at me but I'd lost everything. I'd lost the company. I'd lost my money that I'd had in the company. I'd lost my job, my salary. I'd lost everything."

"What made me hold my hand up? Because I'd gone as low as I could get. In myself, you know ... I thought 'That's it. Better hold my hand up. Come out and tell.' The trigger was thinking about topping myself. That was my trigger."

Click onto the business book section of Amazon, or any similar book based emporium, and you will find hundreds of titles along the lines of 'How to Make a Million Dollars in 10 days', 'The Pathway to Success' or 'The Ten Things You Need to Rule the Business World.'

And they are all written by multi-millionaires with several global businesses who spend their time wandering the earth, telling people how great you can be as long as you work hard and subscribe to their next DVD. They are perceived by general society as being 'successes'.

And that's fine. You should read those books. Copying successful people is, as they say, the best way to succeed yourself and these guys know how to do it well.

However...

That's all very well if you are in the corporate rainforest trying to climb as high up the tree as you possibly can. But what about if you've just fallen off your tree and landed in a pit of quicksand?

Who would you rather get help from in that situation? The guy perched at the top of the highest tree who can tell you how to avoid the quicksand? Or the person stood nearby; with bleeding fingers because they've just clawed their own way out?

When you are in the pit, your prime objective is to

get onto solid ground. You can worry about climbing the trees at a later date.

When I was at school, I remember being taught a very difficult, complicated subject. It was quite a large subject, so we had two teachers covering different bits of the syllabus. One of the teachers was an experienced, incredibly clever teacher, with a first from Oxford in the very subject that they were teaching. The other was not long out of training with a reasonable degree from A.N. Other University.

That year, I learnt far more from the inexperienced, supposedly "less intelligent", teacher.

Why?

Because the first teacher was good at the subject. Excellent in fact. It came naturally to them, so they found it easy and couldn't understand why we were struggling with the concepts.

Whereas the second teacher didn't find it quite so easy. They knew what issues we were having, because they had had the same problems themselves. And they knew how to overcome them, in a way that we could relate to.

And that's where this book comes in. The ideas and thoughts contained herein have been shaped and sourced directly from people who would be perceived by general society as 'failures'.

They include people who have seen their marriages torn apart; been threatened in the street by angry creditors; hidden behind closed curtains waiting for the bailiffs to go away; and sunk into the depths of depression, causing them to hide from the world for months on end.

But they survived.

That in itself makes them a success.

More than that, they also want to help others who may be facing similar situations.

Now, I'm not going to promise that by reading this book, you will automatically be able to rescue your business (assuming it is in trouble). But what it will do is give you the best chance to save it. To help you stay focused, determine your priorities and make tough decisions based on logic and not emotion.

And if your business does fail, you need to be able to deal with the realities of the situation, work out what you're going to do next and get on with it as quickly as you can.

Then you can start to look at climbing the trees.

> *"When you're saying 'Do you think you are offered the support mentally?' I think that is an extremely valid point and I would say 'Definitely not!' At no stage has anybody, and I'm not blaming anybody, at no stage has anybody ever*

considered the mental state of the directors or the wellbeing of the directors. I did find that very difficult and I also found it amazing that the biggest asset that the firm had was, in effect, myself and the senior team and that asset was just, really, abused.

I think that is a massive area that needs to be looked at going forward, isn't it? And the country needs profit and wealth creators and just destroying them like that doesn't actually help anybody."

HOW TO READ THIS BOOK

It is important that you approach this book in the right way if you are going to the get the most benefit out of it.

First of all, whilst this book is set within an English business context, the key focus is on the human element. Consequently, I believe that the key concepts are relevant to any business owner, regardless of country.

Secondly, the intention of the book is to generate ideas in your mind, see things from a different point of view and, hopefully, produce action points that will help you in your situation.

No individual person is in exactly the same situation or space as another, so I can't be specific and prescriptive about the action each person should take. For some, they will have all the information they need by the end of Chapter 2. For others, they won't even become interested until near the end of the book.

However, I believe that every section has the potential to provide something of interest and of use, regardless of your context.

You may, therefore, want to come back to the book several times to get the full benefit. However, for the first read, you will get more out of it if you follow it in the order it is written.

Included within the book are certain exercises that it is recommend you have a go at. Some of these build up over the course of the book so, again, following it in order will be of greater benefit.

In addition to the order that you read it in, you also need to find some time and space.

If your business is in trouble you are more than likely going to be running around like a lunatic trying to sort things out.

You will see that one of the recommendations that fell out of the interviews is that you take some time out of your business in order to avoid brain burn out.

You have the book. Make use of it.

- Reserve half an hour a day or an hour at weekends, to read a chapter or two.

- Find a quiet space where you won't be disturbed.

- Have a pen and paper to hand. Some of the activities require these, but you may also find thoughts and ideas coming to mind as you read things. It is always best to jot these down before you forget them.

Once you have covered the contents of the book

you will hopefully have a different perspective on things and have some definitive action points that will help you.

At the end of the book is a Glossary, which contains an explanation of the more common terms that you may not be familiar with.

In addition, there is further information that can be downloaded from my website. Practical business tips from the contributors and an explanation of what actually happens in an insolvency are both freely available at:

www.businessenjoyment.com/books

So, get that pen and paper, make yourself comfortable and I wish you good reading.

CAVEAT

This book is **NOT** a solution for extreme situations such as clinical depression or suicidal tendencies.

Whilst one or two of the contributors have experienced these situations and some reference is made to them, no one involved with its publication has any training or qualifications in such areas.

If you, or someone you know, is experiencing such issues then you must seek assistance from an appropriately qualified professional.

CHAPTER 1 : TWO TYPES OF STRESS

> *"There was two types of stress really. There was the stress of actually going through the liquidation and there was the stress of "What am I gonna do next?*
>
> *And the most stressful thing, I think, of all, was "What am I gonna do next?"*

In all businesses, large or small, successful or struggling, there are two fundamental elements.

There is the business itself: the product; the processes; the systems; the numbers; the assets etc etc.

And there are the people.

Whilst there are numerous mechanised processes and automatic systems that can be put in place, there is not a single company or trade in the world that has completely removed the human element.

In particular, there is always someone at the top.

A person. A human being that has to make decisions regarding strategy and directional changes in response to market forces. A human being that has to make tough decisions at difficult times. A human being that can be influenced by emotions, feelings of stress and levels of self-confidence.

A human being that can make mistakes.
The Business Cycle

The life cycle of a business can be easily mapped out and, whilst time scales can alter, every business will go through the same recognisable phases.

In the initial period of a business's life, we have the Start up Phase, The Growth Phase and the Mature Phase. From there, performance can vary but tends to fluctuate as though it were on a rollercoaster.

However, in this book, we are looking at the end of a business's life.

The beginning of the end will start with a CRITICAL EVENT (see Fig. 1).

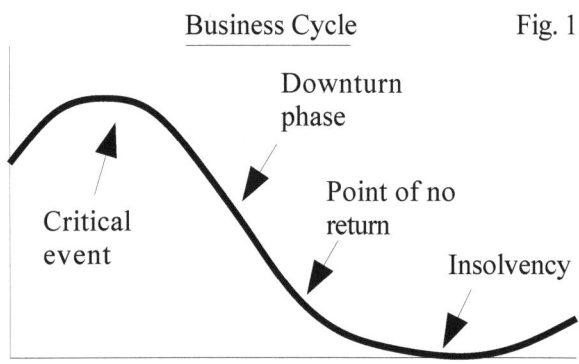

This may be clear and obvious, such as a major customer going bust and wiping out your cashflow. However, it could also be a number of more subtle things that have all come together at the wrong time. It may be the opening of a factory in China which, in time, will take away all your customers. Or a combination of increased online shopping and supermarket dominance that leads to your high street shop getting less passing trade.

Whatever it is, and regardless of how identifiable it is at the time, eventually it will lead to one of those rollercoaster dips continuing a bit too far and we will be in to the DOWNTURN phase.

If this downward progression continues without being checked, we start approaching THE POINT OF NO RETURN.

From hereon in, there is no way of escaping and INSOLVENCY becomes inevitable. Note, however, that insolvency isn't always an instant process. The run in can last anywhere from days to months.

In some cases, everything ends here. However, it is possible for the business to resurrect itself post-insolvency and the whole life cycle can begin again via the Start up Phase.

So. All fairly straightforward and, barring the odd minor detail or point of terminology, nothing that shouldn't be obvious to most people.

And, because this life cycle is easily recognised and established, there is an entire industry of external professionals around, set up to help the business at every single stage of that cycle.

In general, we are talking about Company Doctors, Turnaround Directors, Corporate Restructuring and Insolvency Practitioners. And, with their support, the business can either be saved or, if that isn't possible, wound down in the most appropriate manner.

That's the business side of things.

But what about the people side of things?

The Personal Cycle

Whilst there are layers of support for the business, what is going on with the person in charge? That human being that is being influenced by emotions, stress and self-confidence?

This person follows a different curve.

Firstly, there will be the point where the individual SHOULD (see Fig. 2) be aware that there is something wrong. However, it is natural to blank these things out at first and live in a state of denial, so we tend not to do what we should do.

> *"I think first of all you've got to admit you've got a problem. I think it's the same as an alcoholic. If you can't admit it, you're never going to come out of it. You're just gonna do what you've always done."*

Then we get to the point when the penny drops and they DO know that something is wrong. Up until now, stress has been slowly increasing and the self-confidence chipping away. Once we hit this trigger point, there is likely to be a marked shift in both elements (in the wrong direction, naturally).

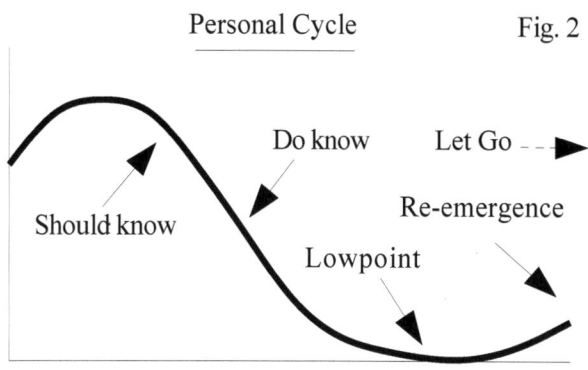

Emotions will be in turmoil and there will be combinations of anger, panic and uncertainty and the ability to think clearly and make crucial decisions is hampered dramatically.

> *"You hang, in those moments, on the positive bits and you tend to ignore the rest. So even though I can go into a meeting with the bank appointed accountant and he'll say 'This could end up in administration or liquidation.' You're like 'Yeah, it could do.'*

It's almost like going to the doctors saying you could drop dead with a heart attack next week or you could live to 80. So you hear it as, 'Yeah well, I could get struck by lightning and I could have a heart attack next week or I could live till 80'. So you think 'On balance of probabilities, I'm going to live maybe to 70.' So you don't quite take it to the 80 mark. You always put it back a little bit."

Eventually, the individual will hit the LOWPOINT. How low this is and how long it lasts will depend on the individual, but there will be such a point for everyone.

From here, the individual will start to rebuild. It is not uncommon to hide away following the LOWPOINT and so I call the next critical step the point of RE-EMERGENCE.

The trajectory from here depends on the depth of the LOWPOINT and the speed of RE-EMERGENCE. Eventually there will be the point at which they can LET GO, although not everyone reaches this stage and their ongoing performance and confidence levels can be permanently scarred by their earlier experiences.

Comparing the curves

Now, at first glance, the two curves seem very similar. However, whilst the two curves may influence each other, there is no direct causality. In other words, the timing of the key stages of the individual may be completely different from that of the business.

Some people whip through the personal curve at high speed and are on their feet with a new business up and running before the ink is even dry on the insolvency appointment documents.

Most people aren't quite so quick. In some cases, the penny doesn't really drop until after the business has shut down and they are home alone without a job and no plan for the future.

What is critical is that both elements are recognised and dealt with, as both parts are in need of support.

Support for your Business

> *"There's no need in this day and age. There is no need to do what happened to me. There are so many people out there that want to help organisations. But people, sometimes ... you can't ... they just won't listen."*

I want to make this very clear. If you want support for your business, there are literally thousands of companies out there to help you.

Yes, it will cost money. Yes, you have to decide which one to use. Yes, it will interrupt the natural flow of your current operations.

But, it doesn't matter if you are a sole trader or a multi-national conglomerate, never say that the support isn't there.

> *"I have learnt, at the end of the day .. there are very good people out there, and there are people waiting to help you. It's just you've never got together with them."*

Furthermore, there are hundreds of books and websites that can give you good advice and suggestions on how to increase sales, diversify, reduce costs and generally get the best out of your business.

This book is not one of those.

Practical business tips

Naturally, as I spoke to the different business people and asked them what they had learnt via hindsight, a number of practical things about how you should structure your business fell out.

Granted, these particular points are not of much use when you are already in trouble. In much the same way, a discussion about increasing the number of lifeboats on the Titanic is important and pertinent, but not much use when you're treading water in the Atlantic.

If, however, you are interested to see what sort of practical tips cameo out of these discussions, then you can download them for free on my website:

www.businessenjoyment.com/books

On the other hand, if you are already sinking and want some urgent advice on what to do, the following may help:

1. Go through your balance sheet and look for any assets that can be converted into cash (spare assets, debtors, vehicles etc).

2. Go through your cash flow forecast and, for every entry, think about ways of increasing and speeding up cash coming in – and reducing or delaying payments going out.

Be careful that you don't do anything illegal, like avoiding tax payments. This is another reason for having a professional advisor alongside you, especially for major decisions.

For smaller businesses struggling to pay off their creditors in full, I'll hand you over to one of the contributors.

> *"Write everything down. All the bills - and then work at the first one. Say, 'Right, I've earned twenty quid this week. I'm going to give him a fiver, the next person a fiver, the next person a fiver, the next person a fiver.' And then the next twenty quid you earn, go to the next person and the next person. And then come back*

round to your first person. Right, I've got another twenty quid.

And the target is to go through things very logically. Don't worry about who they are, just write them down on a bit of paper and say 'Right, you've got to start at paying somebody something out of it.' Or, even if it's the first one, paying 10%, the next one 10% - but just paying something off. Everybody equally. Somewhere along the line. And doing that consistently and just ploughing at it. Ploughing at it and you'll get through it.

Don't say 'Oh God! I'll never earn that money and I'll never get there.' Don't do that. And you can get through anything if you plough at things."

But, I repeat, this book is not here to provide you with that practical business support. If you really need help in fundamentally restructuring how your business looks, or suspect that you are close to being technically insolvent, then you need to get professional advice.

IMPORTANT NOTE: It is a legal requirement for directors, as soon as they suspect that the company cannot avoid an insolvency, to consult a licensed insolvency practitioner. Carrying on regardless can be deemed Wrongful Trading, which can lead to fines and disqualification as a director.

Now, the thing is, once you get some support for your business, that is only half of the story.

What you will discover is that the business support that is out there is literally that. Support for your business. Not you.

There are some very good professionals, who will put their arm around you and tell you it will be all right and they'll help you make the right decisions. Some of them even care about what happens to you.

But it's not their JOB to help YOU.

They won't be able to help you deal with the stress of worrying about the personal guarantee you gave the bank; the crumbling marriage due to the strain of it all and the two hours sleep every night meaning that you are exhausted each morning and in no mood to face another day of angry calls and demands for information.

> *"From a business point of view, we did talk to a couple of people about a recovery/turnaround. Spent a lot of time investigating our market and processes. There was some advice and input but I don't think that, just as a person...as an individual...I was ready to talk about it. I was sort of doing it almost objectively. It was just talking about the business, it wasn't talking about me and I was all at sea really. You know. I*

> *was ... erm ... really really low self esteem was the big characteristic of it"*

Now. I believe that if the business has not yet reached the point of no return then, as long as the director is in the right personal space, then they are capable of turning it around themselves.

Even if that doesn't happen, the director is still someone likely to create a new business in the future. In order for that to happen as quickly as possible, they need to come through the ordeal as unscathed as possible.

Consequently, the director needs personal support as much, if not more than, the business support.

Support for the individual

> *"I could have done with somebody to show me the way through. There was a business part, and I had someone to help me there. And there was the 'What am I going to do next?' part. That is where someone could have helped."*

So where can you get support for yourself? Someone to help you stay focussed, keep in control and minimise the impact that the emotions are having on your decision making abilities.

Family and Friends (?)

The first area of consideration should be family and

friends. However, this may not be a straightforward solution, hence the question mark.

> "When you run your own company, you're pretty independent anyway, so I didn't have the closeness of friends that would have particularly offered any support. And with friends, it's very difficult to get support anyway in a lot of situations. Sometimes it's just sympathy you get, not support."

Furthermore, it can often be hardest to open up to those that are closest to you. The closer you are, the harder it can sometimes be for them to be objective.

> "One or two of them said 'Well, you'll just have to get a job...Tesco's, won't you?' type of advice. Which was fine, but...there was a little undercurrent of almost 'and that serves you right, doesn't it?' feeling, you know?"

Or in the other direction:

> "It's a cliché and you don't think you're doing it at the time, but they tell you don't listen to what your friends and family tell you 'cos they're only telling you what you want to hear. 'Cos they've got your best interests at heart."

However, your first thought should be those that are closest to you and consider whether there is anyone that you would be happy to talk to.

Be confident that they would be able to give you good answers. Particularly answers you don't want to hear. If they tell you something that makes you feel uncomfortable, then they are doing the right thing.

> *"I think friends daren't say something to you that really would be wise to have said a few years earlier. You know, let you know that you're going in the wrong direction.*
>
> *And I don't think we like to say that to people. You don't like to point out somebody's faults, do you? And I think that is the hard thing. You got to learn to point out your own faults, which we ignore tremendously.*
>
> *'Cos no matter how good a business is, something could have worked a little better. If you'd looked at it earlier, a little bit sooner."*

Trusted advisor

The next type of person to consider is a trusted advisor.

> *"I'd ask for help, because it's not a sign of weakness, is it? And probably go to the right people. Not the people around me. And that's something I've learnt over the last 5 or 6 years. People are experts because they're experts. You know, your friends and family and your workmates, they're not EXPERTS at certain*

> *things. Go to the experts.*
>
> *Don't try to cut corners and think you can do everything. If someone is qualified to do something that I can't do, you pay that person to do it. Because anything else ... you're short changing yourself really."*

Someone that you already interact with on a business level and someone you have faith in. Your accountant, your solicitor or just a very good business person that you know and whose opinion you respect.

> *"Probably the best advice I was getting was from the solicitor. He was probably pretty much on my side. He would have been the person I would have listened to more.*
>
> *He had a very balanced, experienced view. He knows that there are people out there that are complete shysters. He took a more rounded view so he started to look after my position rather than just purely the company position.*
>
> *I think somebody that's not just looking after the business, but looking out for you as well, as an individual, can see your circumstances, can see what your life was, who you're engaged to – looking at it all round. I think somebody in that position is better."*

However, as alluded to earlier, how far can they

actually provide you with that extra level of support? The previous commentator continues:

> *"But, he was a commercial solicitor, he wasn't somebody looking out for you all round. He just gave a little bit more than some of the others did."*

So, check your contacts and people of trust and see who you think it would be worth talking to. But look for people that will be able to give that little bit extra time - and view you as more than just someone that runs a business.

It's good to talk

> *"Talk to somebody. Yeah. Talk to somebody. Because it ... this is probably a bit of a cliché, but it oughtn't be ... it might only be one sentence or one remark ... a throw away thing ... that opens a door. 'Cos all you're doing is going round and round in circles and there's no answer. You think you're going to come up with the answer, but all you've got for a frame of reference is what you've been involved in. And it can sometimes feel quite closed and claustrophobic, you know? Dead ends everywhere.*
>
> *Yeah, I think it starts with just being able to get the problems out. I can imagine that being quite cathartic and if I put myself back in that*

> *position ... yeah, to be able to go and talk to somebody and be open and honest and ... you know, I mean it's like today. I think ... I think that's the first ... today is the first time that I've basically admitted out loud that I didn't really want the business to work. Or I wasn't bothered if it worked or not. But from my point of view, today, that's felt like a weight gone. Being able to say that has been liberating really."*

If you're still struggling to find the right person, then just start with someone. Doesn't matter if they know anything about business, as long as they are prepared to lend you an ear, then you have a candidate.

> *"I've always said, if you talk to somebody about it, it does become a little bit easier. To actually tell somebody, what was going on and I think if there were people out there who you could talk to about your business but without....erm not to complain and grumble about it but just somebody that you could actually talk to that did actually kind of understand what business was about and understand about businesses and could actually sympathise that little bit with you."*

Unfortunately, it is human nature for us to take the weight of the world on our own shoulders and extremely difficult to admit to someone that we need help. Particularly men.

> *"I've never been a talker. I don't talk to people about my problems. My problems are my problems. And if I pass my problems to you then you've got my problem and I'd rather do it myself. You know what I mean? And for all my life I've never even told my mother and father anything. It's something I've held in all the time. My [business] partner does that, who I used to work with. And he looks terrible with it. But now I let it go. I talk about it. 'Cos it's out there then. It's gone ain't it?"*

By the way, if you are reading this and you know someone that you think is facing difficulties, it may be that you need to be the one who forces them to take stock. You may be that friend or trusted advisor that they need. At the very least, give them a copy of this book.

> *"I think for anybody, if somebody somewhere who maybe had a fairly brutal conversation....maybe there was somebody on the outside who we knew who was having thoughts of 'They're in a bit of a tricky place.' Maybe if they'd ...a bit like an intervention...somebody who was an alcoholic perhaps or something like that...had sort of sat me down...sat us down and said 'You know what, if you don't do this, this and this, then it's over and if it is over you need to do something*

> *about it now.*
>
> *It might be a bit difficult at the exact time of the conversation...generally I'm a reflector so people say things and I don't necessarily react straight away so I like to digest it a bit and think ... hmm ... that little voice inside that says 'they're right, you know they're right.'"*

Get a coach

The other area that is worth investigating is working with a business coach.

A coach is trained to work with you as an individual and to help you focus on what you want and how to get it. This can include areas such as rebuilding self-confidence, managing your time properly, dealing with stress and gaining clarity on options available - many of the areas where issues can arise at this difficult time.

> *"It does make you look at things in a completely different light. I find it enlightening that as a businessman you ... the angle that they see it from ... you would never get to that.*
>
> *It does mean that you don't become angry. And it does become that you become very matter of fact."*

If you do any networking, you will probably have met quite a few. If you have never really understood what they do, now is the time to get to know them better.

One major benefit of a coach is that they are not impacted by what decisions you make with the business and remain, therefore, independent. An existing professional advisor may see your business as a source of income and so may, even if subconsciously, be biased towards what advice they give.

Many coaches run a free introductory session, so it should be possible to see if it would be of use to you, or test out different ones to see who works with you best.

And, once engaged, they can be a very cost effective way of making progress. I managed to find a way to coach people without it costing them any money at all. It wasn't for free, there was a quid pro quo involved, but it didn't require any actual payment to be made. Other coaches may have similar, inventive payment structures to help in situations where cash is limited.

> *"One of the things that I'm absolutely 100% convinced of, is that everybody, but everybody, needs a coach. They need that outside input. 'Cos you get too close to stuff and you get so you can't see it. Even when people point it out to you, you don't listen. It goes in one ear and out of the other."*

ACTION POINT 1.1 – Get talking and analyse your emotions

Find someone to talk to about what you're going through. Any form of release will be of benefit, but the more structured the support, the better.

What is critical is that, whoever you talk to, their position is not impacted by the route you take with the business. They must be independent.

Continue to read through this book. Hopefully there will be things that make you nod and lead you to take action.

However, whenever you hear or read something that makes you **angry**...stop!

An angry reaction normally masks a weakness or a problem.

So, analyse your angry reactions and be honest with yourself. Work out the underlying reason behind the emotional response.

Now you are finding the deeper areas where you really need support. And when you know where the problems are, it is easier to resolve them.

The following chapters may help you develop action points.

CHAPTER 2 : THE SLIPPERY SLOPE

"It's to do with how you're feeling within yourself. Whether it's getting on top of you or it isn't. So there were probably times when the thought would come in your mind 'If this doesn't get resolved in the next kind of couple of weeks or a month or something...what's going to happen?'

But it's pretty easy for a couple of weeks to go by and then it's like 'Well, okay. It doesn't feel too much worse than it did.' You get a very narrow view. You lose the wider perspective. You can't sort of step out from yourself and view it from beyond. And so, at that point ... when you have a positive conversation with a new customer that might lead to a decent sale you think 'Crikey! Fantastic! It's okay. It'll be okay.' You know?

And you lose a real perspective of what's going on because you're just caught up in it."

Beware the innocent

I have some good news and some bad news.

The bad news is that, if you're going to go down, you will not see your assassin until they strike. Whatever the means of your downfall is, however long it takes and no matter the form, you won't see it until it is too late. Or, if very lucky, <u>almost</u> too late.

> *"You get the odd little clue prior to that, so we had a clue about in the June, before the September. There were no visible signs outside of that. As soon as Northern Rock happened, it was the answer to what was happening. It was like 'There's something strange happening, but we don't know what.' and then it's 'A-ha. That's what's happening'. ".*

And the event that triggered it all will have happened a long time ago and will either be something completely out of your control, or something so small that you gave it no heed at the time. Take, for example, some of the situations that the contributors found themselves in.

- Taking on a large profitable contract which led to them relying too much on one customer and being too lenient on that customer's account, until one day they found out the customer had gone bust owing them a death dealing debt.

- Failing to spot a shift in the market, that started a couple of years ago but took a while to have an impact on the numbers, by which time it was impossible to do anything about it.

- Not giving enough attention to local politics and by-laws which led to an innocuous letter from the council to discuss the finer details of planning permission, and ended up killing the business as it could no longer carry on doing what it did.

- Or, of course, ignoring a shift in general corporate culture towards short term gains versus long term profits leading to increased levels of borrowing and the pursuit of riskier investments, ultimately ending up in a major property crash and a double dip recession.

The final blow may be severe, but its roots will have come from something you didn't see at the time.

So, what's the good news then?

Well, the good news is that you have two ways of covering it off.

Firstly, you have the all encompassing, pro-active approach.

When setting up your business, anticipate every single possible event that could ever happen in the future of the world and build in contingencies accordingly. And after a year of doing planning and installing, you might be able to actually start running your business. Assuming, that is, that the many layers of red tape you've installed allows you to do so.

Alternatively, recognise that you can only do so much; use common sense and standard practices to install a reasonable amount of caution and safeguard and keep your fingers crossed.

At the end of a horse race, it's obvious which horse you should have bet on. By Saturday evening, you know which Lotto numbers you should have picked this week. If you bet on every horse or select every number, you can guarantee a win but won't actually make any money.

So, if an event should happen in your business, don't waste time beating yourself up about what you should or shouldn't have done. Just get on with dealing with the consequences.

Oh, and even greater news! Because of the times we live in, you have the best get out clause ever. Simply blame everything on the recession and take away any personal guilt.

That may seem a bit facetious, but it is very difficult for people to admit that things aren't working and to ask for help. We'll look at this in more detail later, but what better way to shift any guilt and blame from yourself than to use a global event that has affected everyone?

And don't worry if you think that it's too late to use that excuse. Any intervening years between the crash and now are just an illustration of how well you've done to keep things going for this long.

ACTION POINT 2.1 – Reserve some reflecting time

I am making an assumption that you are reading this book because something has happened in your business.

Either it is something small: itching and scratching away at you and giving you a sinking feeling deep down that all is 'not right'.

Or it is something massive that has completely wrecked your future trade.

Or something in between.

If you are spending time agonising over what went wrong and what mistakes you made, I want you to do the following.

Get out your calendar or diary, or whatever you use to track appointments.

Find a free day in about a month's time. Make it a weekend if you like. But block out that day and make sure you keep it free.

And label that day as a "Business reflection day" or whatever title you prefer.

And you are going to spend that day going over everything that happened that led to whatever the event was; everything that you did to prevent it from happening; and everything else that you could have done.

Now that you have a day in the future dedicated to such considerations, you don't need to spend any time on it before then and can focus on what needs to be done now to recover the situation.

And that includes coming up with whatever excuse you need, that will make you feel comfortable enough to ask for help.

And the quicker you do that, the better.

Death by a thousand cuts

> *"You don't realise it yet but you will die. You won't die suddenly. You will die a slow death. You will get sliced slowly on many occasions and you will bleed to death."*

Not everyone faces the same business curve. In some cases the incident is so swift and significant that there is very little that you can do. I've spoken to people who have discovered a major fraud or had a significant debtor go bad on them and they've known almost immediately that they are insolvent, with an appointment happening within a week.

However, others face a more gentle slope into oblivion. I mentioned earlier about the concept of a rollercoaster dip turning into a DOWNTURN and it is very difficult to spot the point where one becomes the other. Only in hindsight does it ultimately become obvious.

> *"It begins with compromises in your life style that you think 'Well, that's okay. I don't mind doing that. Going to cheaper supermarkets etc. And then it becomes 'Are we going on holiday this year?' And it's 'Hmm. Don't know. Depends on how things go with the business.'*
>
> *And so there's this little erosion. Gradually."*

Where you have this slow decline, then you have a much longer period in which it is possible to rescue the business and turn it around, avoiding insolvency.

Unfortunately, there is the personal curve to take into consideration and that period of denial between SHOULD know and DO know becomes the overriding factor that determines whether the business will survive or not.

The type of pattern often goes something like this:

Down – **Up** – **Down** – **Up** – **Down** – **Down** – *Gosh, tough month* – **Down** – *Another tough one. How disappointing* – **Down** - *Should take action but believe it'll be fine* – **Down** – *Maybe it's getting a bit tough now* – **Tiny up** – *Ah, that's better. All sorted now* – **Down** – *Damn!* - **Down** – *Really ought to do something now* – **Down** – *Right, definitely going to do something* – **Down** – *Help!* - *Oh, too late.*

The combination of the two different curves means that, frequently, nothing happens during that critical period where business rescue is possible. Once the penny has dropped it is too late and rescuing the business becomes very difficult indeed.

A major part of the problem is down to evolution.

Scientists have demonstrated that, subconsciously, we are actually an optimistic bunch. Despite evidence that categorically demonstrates things to the contrary, we go about life convinced that we won't contract a major illness, have an accident or be the victim of a crime.

We may moan and grumble and talk about expecting the worst, but we still behave as though nothing really horrible will befall us.

And if we were to behave in any other way, then we'd never get out of bed.

If you trace things back to our ancestors, we lived in a brutal and violent world. Every foray for food could result in injury or death, either from an animal we were hunting fighting for its life or from another predator hunting us.

The risk averse creatures that hid, scurried and cowered, evolved into the mice and voles of the world. We evolved from the animals that took risks and got on with things irrespective of the dangers that we were faced with.

Consequently, we now only actively react to danger when there is an immediate threat to life.

We send ourselves little warning signs, which come across as feelings of fear and trepidation. These are there to keep us on our toes. But action is only taken when the tipping point is reached and the evidence has become so overwhelming that we can't ignore it any longer.

In today's corporate world, where physical threat is a rarity, our senses are ill suited and so we don't take action when we should. Ironically, we still hold the sense of fear, but more of that later on.

> *"You don't realise how much pressure you're under sometimes until the pressure is lifted."*

And this slow, drawn out descent into oblivion can be more damaging to the individual.

Every day there's another disappointment and every disappointment slices away another bit of self confidence and self esteem.

> *"So my confidence was, you know,...just chipping away, chipping away, chipping away. And the longer that went on it just went lower and lower and lower to a point where there's probably this break-even point where it's like 'Oi! Have a word with yourself. You need to hold your hands up. Admit some things."*

Now the trouble is, that "break-even point" referred to above, comes at different times for different people. One person I asked as to when the penny dropped responded with this.

> *"I think when ... we had some electric gates. They just came along with the house..when we got the house. That meant that people had to buzz at the gate. When some of those people were bailiffs and you weren't sure if they were bailiffs and you were literally just sort of peering out from behind the curtain thinking 'Is it safe to let them in?' That's probably when... in the dead of night when you're still awake you start thinking 'Hmm. This might be beyond redemption.'"*

Only those people who have been through the situation can appreciate how easy it is to take things so far without fully realising. How hard it is to step outside the box and see what is really going on.

The mind is a strange thing and it can only take so much pressure.

> *"We definitely went through a phase, when things were hard, of actively not thinking about stuff. We hid it away. So we watched the whole six seasons of The Sopranos.*
>
> *A lot of it was us engaging the head and the brain into something so that we didn't have to*

> *think about the other stuff. It was a need to stop thinking about it all the time. It was a need to do something to just ... switch off because my wife and I just lost weight and lost sleep and lost confidence and, you know, it was just a way to do something to lose your train of thought."*

As mentioned, by the time you get to this stage, it is pretty much too late for the business, no matter what help you seek. Remember the quote in Chapter 1 from the person that sought help from some turnaround professionals, but, personally, wasn't in a place to take on board their advice? Those last two quotes are from the same person.

However, more importantly, is the time it takes for the individuals concerned to get back on their feet. Generally, those that accepted there was a problem early on and took appropriate steps, found themselves with another business or some form of employment very quickly.

Whereas those that suffered from a drawn out affair were looking at around 12 to 18 months before they were in a place where they were prepared to go again.

That is a long time out of action.

How can I tell a dip from a downturn?

What is clear is that it isn't easy.

As mentioned earlier, we can't account for every eventuality and we're programmed not to act on what we suspect, anyway. So, how can we possibly detect when there's a problem?

> *"You know, sales tend to be, you know, sawtooth or rollercoaster ... but you just thought it was a natural progression. You know, 'We're on a downer'. But it just never picked up."*

Well, as with many things, it's a combination of planning, awareness and common sense.

ACTION POINT 2.2 – Do some market research

In any period of poor performance, you have to establish whether this is something that is happening to just you, or whether it is a wider issue. And I don't mean by just reading the newspapers. Really delve into your specific market and check out your competition.

> *"The realisation came when I saw the financial indexes of the bigger companies ... and they were on the way down ... and it was that. That actually had an effect on me and I said 'Look. It's not just us.'*

> *Because we'd had a reasonably healthy company for 13 years. And there was bits of, you know, cashflow issues which ... erm, the bank saw us as a healthy company as well because we didn't have all our eggs in one basket. We'd got a spread of lots of different clients. But when sales just weren't coming, it kept going, kept going ... then we realised that we'd reached the point of no return."*

If it is just you and the market still exists, then you should be looking at what steps you can take to tap into that market in a different and better way than you are now.

If the market is changing, then you need to change with it.

If the market is shrinking, then you need to find a new market to get into.

> *"It was the fact that things were shrinking and we weren't seeing it at all. We weren't noticing the bigger picture. We were just seeing our own little area and we weren't going any further than that. I think that's because we didn't get out enough and look around enough. We didn't have contact with people enough to realise that they were in the same boat as us. You just blame yourself all the time.*
>
> *There's a pattern to everything. And it goes*

> *round in that pattern. You know...and you just have to watch that pattern shifting. And, hopefully, see it quick enough to shift with it."*

ACTION POINT 2.3 – Put some measures in place

> *"You've got to put some measures in. And one of the measures is your own personal stability, financially.*
>
> *So, if something happens to me tomorrow, where are we financially?*
>
> *So, that means looking at what income's coming in and if it isn't coming in ... in enough amount to meet the basics, then be brutal about how long that is sustainable for."*

Stop and think about what a downturn might mean to you, how it would affect you financially and create some sort of measure that will be your trigger point to ask for help. Obviously not too late. If your measure is something like 'unable to pay the wages', then you've probably got it a bit wrong.

> *"I think the minute that there's any doubt then that's when you start. The minute there's any doubt at all as to the longevity of it. Or, you know, where are you gonna be in 4 weeks time? That's when you start to be honest with yourself and, erm, yeah. Then!*
>
> *Don't ignore it!"*

It depends on your business, but it may be something like the level of your cash reserves falling below a certain point; sales below a key level three months in a row or once below a really low level. Or it may be tied into your own personal finances.

But you need to set up a logical trigger point in advance and a subsequent action plan so that you can remove emotion and evolution from the equation.

> *"As soon as you think 'Okay, the tenants have paid the rent' and you **don't** pay it into the bank account to cover the mortgage going out.*
>
> *Although you know that's what you've done, you think 'Right, okay. So we've got to buy some food, we've got to do whatever.' You start this sort of merry-go-round of juggling, of not enough money to meet everything.*
>
> *That's when your trajectory starts to dip and you start to go downhill."*

ACTION POINT 2.4 – Get into good habits

This one is for those of you that are doing fine at the moment but realise that things may get rocky in the future and you want to be in the best position to deal with it should it happen.

We've talked before about talking to someone, preferably with a bit of business knowledge. A business coach or an experienced friend.

Start using them now, when your business is building or doing well. Because if you get into the habit of talking to people in an open and honest way now – then you will find it a damn site easier to pick the phone up at the first sign of trouble.

> *"There's a lot of value to outside help that you kind of can't put a price on until you've been in a situation where you realise you needed it. I would go for coaching because ... it works. It's as simple as that."*

Summary

Spotting where a dip becomes a downturn is not easy.

However, if you keep an eye on what's happening with others, build in some parameters that are important to you and get into the habit of asking for help at all times, you will put yourself in the best position to ride it out.

But don't waste time exploring reasons and causes. Action is more important than reflection.

Taking that action as quickly as possible is the theme of our next chapter.

CHAPTER 3 : THE INACTION TRAP

> *"Act now because you'll just get more and more miserable and ... you're kidding yourself.*
>
> *Burying your head in the sand doesn't do anything. It just prolongs the inevitable, makes you more miserable and you'll be in the same position anyway. So sort it out today, not 3 months down the line when nothing's changed and you're looking back and thinking 'Well, I should have done this 3 months ago.' Because it's a waste of time."*

In the previous chapter we looked at why people may not notice that there is something wrong. Through a combination of not spotting the signs and personal denial, it is very easy to roll on, despite suspecting that things aren't right. And this can have a serious impact on the ability to rescue the business.

However, even when the penny starts to drop, it can still be difficult to take action. And this can have a serious impact on the personal side of things.

Reasons for inaction

There are many reasons why people hold off from taking action.

> *"There was a lot of fear. And the way I am, I*

> *always try stuff anyway. And I'm quite tenacious and stubborn. I fought to keep it because it's my nature and it was 'what else am I gonna do?' I didn't know that at the time, it's only with hindsight.*
>
> *So I was fighting to keep it because I didn't really know anything else.*
>
> *But going back on it, I wouldn't do it again. I'd have done it straight away."*

A combination of fear and lacking the bigger picture can have a real impact on your ability to take action.

> *"I was just too close to it. I didn't see it and it was passing me by. It was there but it wasn't really brought into the open. Perhaps I didn't want it to come into the open. Perhaps I just couldn't cope with it. You know, it was quite a stressful time."*

Probably the most favourite tactic for delaying action is the belief that something will come up and it will all be right in the end. Also known as 'The Lottery Approach'.

> *"We needed to downsize because of the way the economy was. And we didn't downsize quick enough. And as a consequence we had to put the company into liquidation.*
>
> *There were 10 of us in the company but we*

> *really needed to downsize to like, 4. Something like that, to actually make it work. If we'd gone straight to 4 people we probably would have survived. But we didn't.*
>
> *You're always hoping ... that things would get better ... and you keep struggling on thinking 'Yeah, we'll get a big sale. Get a big contract.' And it just didn't happen.*
>
> *But we put it off as long and as long and as long as we could, which was the worst thing we could have done. Because the pressure at that time was unbelievable."*

Yes, the promise of a new client just on the point of signing a major contract. A new venture which everyone says will make lots of money, just as soon as the ball starts rolling. The passing trade which is bound to pick up any time soon, despite all evidence to the contrary.

Plus, of course, we are always told to think positively and positive things will happen.

> *"There are so many people that you'll say 'How's business?'*
>
> *'Oh great!. Wonderful! I'm doing fabulous!' And they're doing absolutely crap.*
>
> *But you've got to keep saying 'wonderful' to make your own spirits stay there with it.*

> *Because you do truthfully think that it is going to be better tomorrow."*

A combination of the inherent optimism and the refusal to accept that there is a deep seated problem.

> *"You do feel it ... but you always think that you can pull yourself out of it. Because all it needs is one good contract and 'Right. We're back up and running. Let's keep it going.' But it never came."*

The other angle that people find themselves concerned about is that, if they take action too soon it will look like they haven't given it a good enough shot by themselves.

> *"Probably a lot of my problem with it was 'What would my wife think?' You know. 'What would my friends perceive of me?'*
>
> *Even though I knew the business wasn't working ... I'd still go out to the networking events. Still try to make the sales calls. Still do what I needed to on a daily basis to keep it ... I say ticking along, it wasn't really ticking along. I don't know what I did really. But I didn't want to admit to my wife that ... 'cos it ... it's me. It's not the company that used to employ me. It's not this big huge global conglomerate. It's me ... and to have to sort of say ... I didn't want to say*

> *'It's not working. I can't make it work.'*
>
> *'Cos that's admitting that I'm a failure then, isn't it? Because I always felt that ... that she couldn't understand. 'Well, why doesn't it work? Don't be daft. Make it work.'*
>
> *And with a company, I could always blame something, you know. The staff. My boss. The company rules – whatever. But I couldn't make this work and I knew that.*
>
> *I knew that earlier than I admitted. 'I want to get away from it as quick as I can.' But not too quick so people can go 'Well, you didn't give it a go, did you?'*
>
> *And I think if it had been just me, I would have knocked it on the head there and then."*

This leads to a concern that people will think that they gave in too soon and took the easy way out, which makes them appear weak and lack what's needed to be a director or business owner.

> *"In business, you are ... I think you're looked upon to be ... you must know what you're doing and if you don't know what you're doing, that's your fault anyway, so you've made the mistakes. And okay, you have made a mistake, you don't really want somebody to put that mistake right. But you do want to maybe relieve that little bit of pressure that 'I have made a*

> *mistake' and it would be helpful if there was somebody there to actually help you ... not put it right, but not make the same mistake again. And move on in the right way.*
>
> *It would be extremely beneficial to understand you have made a mistake. A lot of the times you deny you've made a mistake, I would think. But at the time, you don't know that. Because you're denying it all the time. That you're not going to get better. That it's never going to get better than it actually has been. In fact, actually, it's going to get worse but you constantly, as I say, every time the bank manager asks you what you're gonna do this year, you always want to exaggerate that.*
>
> *You've got to look at the facts and see where you've gone wrong."*

The cost of delaying

The trouble is, whilst it may cost money to ask for help, the cost of delaying is far higher. And the end result will be no better.

Firstly, there's the additional financial cost. Whilst you try and prop up an ailing company, the size of the creditor base begins to build.

> *"You slowly get behind with the PAYE and the VAT. But we enjoyed such a good relationship with our creditors over a period of time ... they*

> *were fantastic with us. And we always managed to pay them and it was ... it was my wife and myself that did without. We didn't pay ourselves."*

And you end up putting more personal money in to prop it up, usually to pay the higher level of fees, charges and fines you are likely to face from banks and the tax collector.

> *"People were putting us on stop, so I couldn't supply my other customers. I was paying myself something stupid like nine grand a year. That's all I was paying myself. And I was paying my husband the same. And we went months without getting paid because of one customer not paying their debt."*

Secondly, there is the emotional cost. As the process drags on, the stress increases, confidence and self esteem plummets and the greater the tendency becomes that you will make yourself ill and end up putting yourself out of action for months and months.

> *"I think at one stage I ended up with shingles and that got me down quite a bit, because I'd ended up with something that I wasn't in control of and I found that a bit hard, mentally, to actually do it."*

Thirdly, there is the impact on others to take into consideration. It can put greater strain on relationships with friends and family.

> "It's that continuous knot in your stomach, because the pressure is building all the time. It's just that constant gnawing in the back of your mind that's gnawing away at you. The worry of 'Is it gonna get better? Is it gonna get better or is it just gonna get worse?' And it did just get worse and worse. And the pressure ... and the strain it puts on your marriage as well. It puts a hell of a strain on relationships because you don't know what to do for the best."

Employees and subcontractors could end up working harder than ever before and not get paid for their efforts, putting greater stress and financial pressure on them.

> "At some point the realisation just hits you that ... we're at the point of no return. We've got to do something. It's the fact that we know we're not going to have enough money to pay the wages. So you've got to let people go. To make them redundant."

All of this just to maintain face and a bit of pride.

Well, I can assure you that no-one will thank you for it.

ACTION POINT 3.1 - Act now

> *"If it's a dead duck, it's a dead duck. Or if it's failing, you need to act now. Yeah, that would be the first thing. ACT NOW! Because it's not naturally gonna get better. You can't, in most cases, just ride it out and you'd be naïve to do so.*
>
> *Yeah. Act now. Take all emotion out of it and make the decision you know you need to make. Regardless of how painful you think that might be."*

The overwhelming advice from everyone that I spoke to is to act earlier. Whether that is just asking for help or even putting the company down. Act now.

> *"The fundamental mistake was not letting go quick enough. I could have saved myself a lot of heartache at the very very end by doing it a year ... two years before hand.*
>
> *I've learn to be more honest with myself about what I'm doing and where I'm going and what I want to do. Cutting things on the head a bit quicker. Not drawing them out.*
>
> *'Look! Stop kidding yourself that line is going to work. Look, you've had it six months, you haven't sold one. Chop it on the head.*

> *For goodness sake, just learn from your past.'*
>
> *I think that's the biggest thing I would say that I've ... you know. Stop having faith so much. Go on to the next bit. Just let go."*

There is no structured action plan here, I'm afraid. If you can look yourself in the mirror and say with your hand on your heart that everything is fine, then great. But, the fact that you are reading this book suggests otherwise.

> *"Maybe I've learned something with my business which, towards the end of it, which was being open ... you know. Admit sooner. Admit when you should do. You know, don't just soldier on because you're trying to save face.*
>
> *All I was bothered about was how long can I give this ... what's a respectable time to do it for? This needs to end as soon as it can but I've not given it enough of a go yet*
>
> *So I was just counting the days really until I could realistically go 'Do you know what? It's not working. We need to stop it.'*
>
> *It was just about getting to the finish line."*

You need to recognise that there is a problem and that something needs to be done about it.

> *"Now, if I came to somebody with a problem now. Of that magnitude. And they said to me 'I think you should do so & so and so & so and so & so. I'd just do it. My thinking has changed entirely since 2008."*

You have to realise your limitations.

> *"You can't do everything. Eventually, you've got to let go. You can't satisfy everybody. You just can't.*
>
> *So eventually, I thought, 'I'll do what I can do and whatever I can't do, I can't do.'*
>
> *But whatever you do, don't stick with it for too long."*

The best time to ask for help is yesterday.

> *"But if they'd have done it earlier. If someone had told me earlier. 'Don't waste your time! Don't throw any more effort, don't throw any more time into this. Don't work for another two or three weeks without getting paid. Don't incur any more bank charges. Don't do this. Don't do that.' Instead of me being innocent, stupid, young and naïve. If someone would have said 'Cut your losses. Go!'"*

If you didn't ask for help yesterday, ask for it today.

> *"I'd be thinking 'We have to stop ... or make*

changes. We cannot continue just to ... sort of ... go through the same motions.'

Because hope won't pay the wages."

Summary

No-one has ever been criticised for asking for help too early.

If there is any doubt. Any inkling that something is not right. That should be the trigger to do something about it, even if it is just to talk to somebody.

By not taking any action, you start to create problems for yourself. The longer the downturn continues, the closer you get to the point of no return and the fewer options there are available to you and your business.

Eventually, you feel like you've reached a dead end and all you can do is bash your head against a brick wall. However, as we shall see in our next chapter, just because there doesn't appear to be any options available to you, doesn't mean that they aren't there.

CHAPTER 4 : THERE IS ALWAYS A CHOICE

> *"One of the lessons is, there is always a choice.*
>
> *And we could have...even if we didn't feel like it would be worth anything, got a number of other opinions. And who knows, it might...whilst the business may not have continued ... maybe we wouldn't have lost everything. Maybe somebody would have said 'You know what, look, you can't run the business you want to here, so what else can you do?"*
>
> *"But we'd got stuck, or I'd got stuck in 'C'mon, we gotta try and make this work. I don't see how we can do it. What are we gonna do for some income? Oh great, they've just paid the rent. Well, we can probably get away with that for a couple of months."*

If you take only one learning point away from this book, make it this one.

No matter where you are in the process. No matter how much you feel like you are trapped. No matter what you think the situation is.

You do have options.

Much of this is because of the two dimensions highlighted in the first chapter: the business and the personal. Immediately you have two ways of viewing any situation and it may well be that, when there is only one way forward for the business, by focussing on the personal side, more options open up.

Invisible is not non-existent

The other reason as to why there is always a choice is that it is human nature to focus on a problem close up and forget everything around it. By stepping back and looking at the bigger picture or getting another person's point of view, it is not unusual to discover an alternative route.

> *"They will be feeling like there are no options. If there is one thing that they could hear, it would be 'you do have some options.' You can't see them. You don't believe that you have some options, but you do have some options.*
>
> *Talk to somebody who can help you see them. They might just help the perspective widen."*

Getting opinions from other sources is useful as sometimes we just lack the knowledge or awareness of what we can do. We relish the comfort of the familiar and find it difficult to step out of our comfort zone.

> *"I was kind of doing what people do.*
>
> *People don't do what they should. They do what they can. And I wasn't doing what I should, I was doing what I could. So I was fighting to keep it, because I didn't really know anything else."*

And the thought of doing something different doesn't even enter into our heads.

> *"I wasn't open at that time. I was locked into the role of that business that I'd been doing for a long time and I was doing things in a particular way which was not conducive to running a successful business really."*

It is often told: if we do the same things, we get the same outcome.

Consequently, if you are heading in the wrong direction, then you have to make a change.

And be aware that doing nothing is, in itself, the result of a decision.

If you suspect something is wrong, but choose to do nothing about it, or you know you have a difficult decision to make but are putting it off, you are actively making the decision to do nothing.

As long as you are aware that you are making this definitive step and are honestly happy that it is the right thing to do, then fine. But more often than not, we do nothing as a result of fear or lack of understanding.

> *"It's my nature just to think 'It'll be okay. I'll sort it out.' I'm optimistic by nature.*
>
> *But at some point, internally there comes a decision. All right. Stop! That's the point where I think now, if I were in a similar situation, I would go back and say 'what might go wrong?' Even if I can't observe it. Or ask somebody else and say 'look, there's some stuff in this situation that I can't see. I know I can't see it, but because I can't see it, I don't know what it is.'*
>
> *That's probably what I should have done."*

Pick your battles

Another area of choice that you always have is to where you focus your efforts and your energies.

Both of these are going to be in short supply as the pressure mounts and you need to ration them out accordingly. Hard work is not necessarily good work.

> *"We thought we could work harder and we would do better.*
>
> *So we...I suppose, blamed ourselves for maybe not working as hard that year and if we'd worked a little bit harder we could have done a*

> *little bit better. Not realising, actually, it wasn't our fault at all. It was the fact that things were shrinking and we weren't seeing it at all."*

Particularly if hard work is covering a flaw in the business itself.

> *"To some extent, I was blinkered. I meet people now who think that. They think 'Oh! If you work hard it'll come.'*
>
> *No! It's wrong business, it's wrong business."*

Distractions

One danger that people face is that they get easily distracted by issues that are not actually relevant to the matter in hand.

> *"It was probably fuelled by, you know, the extra pressure. It's like anything isn't it. You've probably got so much patience in any one day and so if that patience is being eroded because of another situation..."*

These distractions can come from anywhere. There will be plenty of opportunities at work to find something that will take your focus away from the main objective.

Usually this will manifest itself in a blazing row with an 'incompetent' member of staff or a payment dispute with a supplier.

"Personal problems come out in your business."

But other areas of distraction can be little projects that escalate and escalate. From the search for a decent printing machine that actually works to the development of a new product that will 'change the company's fortunes' at the expense of the existing range.

When you know that there is a big problem to face, the subconscious mind naturally wants to avoid it as there is too much effort and pain attached to it. A smaller, more manageable project is much less scary and it makes you feel like you are achieving something.

Meanwhile, the big problem is just getting bigger.

You can choose where to apply your efforts.

Personal relationships

Distractions also arise at home. The previous quotes, for example, related to an access dispute with a neighbour.

However, the most common area of concern is the risk to personal relationships.

> *"We had quite a good life, I was engaged at the time and we had this quite nice life. We had the horses. We hunted, I did a lot of shooting so it was quite a good life.*

> *Anyway, I got a call from my fiancée one day, she said she wasn't happy. And I came home and the locks had been changed.*
>
> *So I got my clothes and that was it. I didn't get the house, any of the contents. Anything. I just got the clothes that were shoved in her mother's garage and I left and I've not been back since."*

I don't have any current statistics readily available, but I don't think I need to provide any to convince you that it is quite common for a director to experience both a divorce and a business failure within a short space of time.

Which one comes first can vary, as either can cause the other. The downturn of one relationship can lead to a lack of focus on the other.

> *"Unfortunately for me, what happened is, just before the crash I went through a divorce, which was a nightmare. It was a very difficult and acrimonious divorce, so I spent a good three years fighting that."*

And this is where it is vital that you get your personal and your business priorities sorted out. Know what is important to you and what you are prepared to sacrifice for the sake of the other.

Is work more important than family?

> *"Ironically, the best thing ... I was almost prepared for it by going through the divorce. It's almost ridiculous to say, but the divorce and the shit that was thrown at me through the divorce is excellent training for putting your company into administration. 'Cos you realise that actually. Hah! It's nothing compared to having all that thrown at you."*

Knowing what is important to you will allow you to choose where to allocate your resources.

Anger management

At some point you are going to get angry.

It may be as the result of a minor distraction, as alluded to before. Or it may be at the bank for not extending your overdraft and restricting your trading.

There will be plenty of opportunities to rage and rant. And each time will be for a perfectly justifiable reason. And it is perfectly natural in these situations.

And it will get you nowhere.

That's not strictly true. It's actually more likely to send you backwards, as you have a greater chance of raising barriers or burning bridges to people who can help and support you. Or make existing problems worse.

And, as a sentient human being, you have the power to control your emotions.

Subconsciously, you are actually choosing to get angry. You are making a definitive choice to waste time and energy on following a destructive path.

It may not be easy, but you can choose a different path.

Remember Chapter 1. I suggested that whenever something makes you angry, stop and analyse it.

Lying behind that anger is a truth. It will either be a raw nerve that has been hit; a frustration at not being able to see a solution; or a distraction taking you away from the problem that you know that you are going to have to face at some time.

And, because anger is such a focussed point of energy, it is usually targeted at something small – relatively speaking. It may seem massive at the time, but in the great scheme of things it loses its importance.

That's why you need the bigger picture.

ACTION POINT 4.1 – Increase your awareness

Let me re-state some of the issues and frustrations that we've covered in this chapter. They may not all apply to you but, even if you can find just one, this exercise will be useful:

- You feel trapped and there is no way out;

- You think that if you just carry on as normal, things will turn out right in the end;

- You believe that you should have got better results in the last period. If only you'd put more effort in;

- You know that there is a big issue, but you just have to sort a couple of other things out before you tackle it;

- You are arguing more at home and that is affecting you at work;

- People around you are not doing what they should and that annoys you.

Become aware of the potential for these things to happen. Analyse your day and see if any bad points, frustrations or bad emotions you had could mirror one of the things in the list above.

If you do recognise any of them, then remember that you have a choice.

For every single thing on that list there is a different route, a different approach or a different outcome.

Don't worry if you don't see it yet, just accept that there are options to be discovered out there somewhere and be open to looking for them.

In the first instance, think about the situation and come up with just one or two things that you could do differently that would make the overall situation more positive.

You may have to apologise to someone when you're in the right. Stop doing something that you want to do. Or start doing something that you're not comfortable with.

But if it avoids an argument or tackles a big problem, then note it down and save it for later.

ACTION POINT 4.2 – Confirm you are fighting the right battle

> *"Plus I was getting pissed off with it anyway. Doing business with people and running after everyone and it was soul destroying."*

Life progression

Most people treat life like a series of stepping stones where you can only see the ones in front and can only go forward.

We leap onto the first one, have a look at what's in front and jump onto the next. If there are a couple to choose from, then we go with gut feel or avoid the one that looks the most slippery.

When we get to a blockage or an extra long jump, we focus on getting over or across to the next one, without thinking that we can go back and go for an easier route. However, by climbing or jumping, we risk injury or falling in.

All that, and we don't actually know if we'll like what we find on the other side of the barrier.

Is that next stone worth risking yourself for?

If you are fighting to rescue your current situation, let's take a moment to check whether you are fighting the right battle.

Current employment

Grab a piece of paper and write down four headings.

DATE   JOB TITLE   COMPANY   INDUSTRY
(If you are self employed, then use BUSINESS NAME, instead of COMPANY).

Leave a couple of spaces for later, but beneath those headings write: today's date; your current job title; the company you work for; the industry sector you work in.

If you are fighting to keep your business alive, then that is currently what you are fighting for.

Look at it, have a little think about what it means to you and how important it is.

DATE	JOB TITLE	COMPANY	INDUSTRY
-	-	-	-
Today	Managing Director	Myco Ltd	Metal bashing

To the manner born?

Now, presumably, when you were a child, if somebody had asked you what you wanted to be doing when you got to this date, your response would not have been what you've just written down. Probably, if you'd shown that kid the bit of paper you are now looking at, they wouldn't even have understood many of the words.

So there must have been a point when you first wanted to be what you are now.

Have a think about when that was. It might not be that long ago. The first time that you actually wanted to be in the role that you are in now. In the company you are now.

For the record, it is possible to have been actually doing the job for a while before wanting to do it, so don't worry if that is the case.

But when was the moment that you knew that this is what you wanted to be right now?

Back one step

Now, whenever that first moment was, I now want you to think of the DAY BEFORE that moment. A point just before you wanted to do what you are currently doing.

What would your response have been then if

someone had asked you the same question? 'What do you want to be doing when you get to this date?'

What would have been different?

Same company, different job title? Same job title, different company? Or a different industry altogether? Write your answer down on the next line of the table.

The (possibly approximate) date when you last had a desire to do something different and what that desire was – title, company, industry.

If you had no major desire in one of the categories (for example, you always wanted to be a lumberjack, but never cared what level you rose to or which logging company you worked for), then put N/A in the relevant column. But do write in what you did know.

DATE	JOB TITLE	COMPANY	INDUSTRY
-	-	-	-
Today	Managing Director	Myco Ltd	Metal bashing
2 yrs ago	Managing Director	N/A	Metal bashing

Back another step

Now, do the same thing again.

Whatever the previous desire was, when did you first have it. Go back to the day before and think what response you would have given then and write the information down.

Keep doing this until the answer in each column is different from what it is now (Industry is often the last to go here) or you have a full row of N/As.

DATE	JOB TITLE	COMPANY	INDUSTRY
Today	Managing Director	Myco Ltd	Metal bashing
2 yrs ago	Managing Director	N/A	Metal bashing
3 yrs ago	Any Director	Otherco Ltd	Metal bashing
5 yrs ago	Production suprvisor	Otherco Ltd	Metal bashing
25 yrs ago	N/A	N/A	Anything metal related

Back to the future

Now, go back to the top of your list.

Above today's date, write in the date a year from today.

Review your list, how you got to where you are now and how your path has changed along the way.

How important to you is your JOB TITLE?

How critical is it that you have the same title by the same time next year?

Do you actively seek it, or is it just the stepping stone you're currently on?

Remember, you do have a choice.

If you choose to fight for this particular job title, then write it down alongside the date. If not, then write down N/A. (If you have an eye on a more senior position, by the way, then the response is still

N/A, as it is different to your current job).

How important to you is the particular COMPANY you work for?

How critical is it that you have to be in this precise, unique, individual, specific company? Look how long you've been there and how long you've wanted to be there. Think about if you still want to be there.

Is it essential that you stay in this company, or is it just the stepping stone you happen to be on?

Remember, you do have a choice.

If you choose to fight for this specific company, then write it down on the top line there. If not, then write N/A.

Finally, how important is it that you remain in this INDUSTRY?

If you can't imagine doing anything else, just accept the possibility that there are other options out there. You may not know what they are, but they do exist.

Taking that into account, think about what got you into the industry, why you do what you do and what you like about it. And what you don't.

Do you really want to stay in this industry, or is it just the stepping stone you happen to be on?

Remember, you do have a choice.

If you choose to remain in this industry, then write it down. If not, write N/A.

Reassess

So, what are you left with?

If the top two lines (today and next year) are exactly the same, then it looks like you are fighting the right battle.

If you have any N/As in your top line, then you might need to reassess how much energy, emotional as well as physical, you want to be putting into your fight.

DATE	JOB TITLE	COMPANY	INDUSTRY
Next year	N/A	N/A	Anything metal related
Today	Managing Director	Myco Ltd	Metal bashing
2 yrs ago	Managing Director	N/A	Metal bashing
3 yrs ago	Any Director	Otherco Ltd	Metal bashing
5 yrs ago	Production suprvisor	Otherco Ltd	Metal bashing
25 yrs ago	N/A	N/A	Anything metal related

NOTE the word REASSESS. This does NOT mean abandon, give up or ignore.

What it will do is shape your thoughts as we progress.

Knowing where you want to focus your resources will affect what action you take.

ACTION POINT 4.3 – Know why you do what you do

> *"Sit down and really look at why you're in it. Write on a bit of paper your good things about your business and your negative things about your business. Really ask why are you in there? Are you there because you really like doing it? Are you in there just for the money side of it? Really work out, why are you there."*

In the previous exercise, you looked at how important it was to do what you do. Now you need to compare that against everything else in your life.

What's important to you?

So, fresh bit of paper needed and draw a line down the middle of it.

Spend some time to think of all the things that are important to you. As they come to you, write them on the left hand side.

Don't worry about order or level of importance. Just get them down. Think about why you do what you do. Who are you doing it for?.

Project yourself to an ideal future, 30 years from now. Where are you? What are you doing? Who is with you? Who do you still see socially? What hobbies do you have? What charity work do you do?

For example:

> *"If I was to sketch out my perfect week it'd be: ... a round of golf one day; ... go out for lunch with my wife one day during the week; take the kids to watch the football on the weekend ... erm ... and please don't throw things but we bought a caravan at the end of last year and ... you know, just ... to spend some time at the weekend.*
>
> *So there's, you know, there's no Bentleys in there or ... big houses or anything. But it's more about having the time and the choices and the pace of life that I want."*

Anything that you feel is important, put it on the list. Here are some suggestions to get you going:

- Immediate family (partner, kids)
- Remote family (parents, siblings)
- Friends
- Business
- Money
- Employees
- Time
- Playing a sport

- Reading books
- Holidays abroad
- Self esteem

Keep going until you can't think of any more. Then write down another three.

Prioritise

Okay. Now look at each entry on the list in turn and give them a mark out of 10 as to how important they are to you, with 10 being essential.

Make sure that you are marking the thing itself and not what that gets you. So if you give "Money" a mark out of 10 because you need it to pay off the mortgage, then you need to add "Debt free house" on the list and reassess.

Your mark for "Money" should be for the actual ownership of coins, notes or a decent bank balance. Where Money is just a means to something else, then put that something else down.

Review the list and, if you have any items scoring 5 or lower, cross them out.

Once you've done that, transfer the list to the right hand side but, this time, in order of importance with the most important ones at the top. Where you have several entries with the same score, prioritise appropriately.

Introduce a different measure

Now, go down this re-ordered list and give it a **new** mark out of 10. This one represents how much **attention** you are currently giving to it.

So, if you are giving everything you possibly can to that entry, then give it a 10. If you are completely ignoring it and spending no time at all in pursuit of it, then it's a 0.

Time to review

You have listed out what is important to you and how much attention you are giving each thing.

Have you got your priorities right? Are there areas which are getting too much attention and some not getting enough.

Where more attention is needed, think about ONE thing you can do to help improve the situation.

Where you are spending too much attention, think about ONE thing you can do to reduce the amount of attention you give it.

Now go back to ACTION POINT 4.1 and have another look at the items on that list that were relevant to you. What new actions, conclusions or directions open themselves up to you that will help you deal with those situations?

Summary

There's a lot of things to think about here, but if you work through these three steps you should have:

a) a better understanding of your priorities;

b) an idea as to which areas to re-divert some of your energies into; and

c) some definitive action steps to help you move forward.

> *"There is a choice. And back then there was a choice. But I was just...wasn't able to access it. And I'd love to give that message to people who are, you know...for whatever the reasons are...potentially gonna go off that cliff businesswise and personalwise."*

We are now going to focus on an area where someone else may start to call the shots. We will look at the most significant player in the majority of businesses and how they might react to your situation.

The banks!

CHAPTER 5 : DEALING WITH THE BANK

> *"Banks are just knob jocks. You know, they really are stupid. They're not independent at all. You think the banks are going to be on your side, but they're not. They're just completely dictatorial.*
>
> *Do not trust the bank at all."*

Bankers have had a bad press in recent times. In the 1980s they were blamed for overreacting to the financial crisis and busting companies that they didn't need to. This time around they've been blamed for the entire financial crisis itself (conveniently ignoring the part that everyone else played in the whole affair).

So it is very easy, when your company gets into trouble and the bank refuses to give you more money (usage of the word 'give' is deliberate), to use the bank as a scapegoat for your own troubles.

It is a fantastic excuse to lay blame elsewhere.

If only the bank had laid out an extra £250,000 to a company making continual losses with no clear business plan for recovery and no assets to support the debt, it would have been fine.

It's all their fault.

But we need to move away from the blame game. It helps no-one.

> *"The bank was complete and absolutely ... a complete bag of shit. Waste of time.*
>
> *But it was my fault."*

I suggested in Chapter 2 to use the recession as an excuse. Something to blame the demise on. But that was only a short term cover story to give you permission to ask for help. It came hand in hand with time set aside to reflect on what really happened and to find out the REASONS for what occurred.

Don't blame yourself. Don't blame others. Find reasons.

When you understand the reasons, you can learn from them and deal with them. If not this time, then the next time around.

For most businesses, the bank is going to be 'a', if not 'the', major creditor in the process. They are going to have a massive influence on the situation as they have a vested interest in what you do. In fact, it's their money.

So getting angry with the bank (remember what we've said about anger) or ignoring them and hoping they'll go away is not a good strategy.

Understand their reasons. Understand their processes. Deal with them accordingly.

What are banks?

Are they charities that hand out money to deserving people that need it?

Are they not-for-profit organisations with a social conscience?

Are they the corporate equivalent of the welfare state with an obligation to make payments to anyone that turns up with the correct form filled in?

Or

Are they businesses, like you and everyone else, with a duty to make money for their shareholders?

Seems an obvious question and an obvious answer, but it is amazing the number of people that behave as though the answer is one of the first three. They feel that they are entitled to more money from the banks, even though there is no rational reason why anyone would lend it.

You need to think of your bank, not as a partner, not as a friend and definitely not as an open source of money. But for what they are. A supplier. A major supplier, but a supplier nonetheless.

Like any other supplier, they fall over themselves to be nice to you when they think you will buy more things off of them. Like a supplier, they become less friendly if you refuse to pay. (Don't judge. You and I are no different).

It's not a question of being good or evil. It's not anything personal. It's just business.

How they react when things get difficult depends on the bank and it depends on how much you owe them, but let's look at a few situations.

If the bank is not a major creditor

If you only have an overdraft or a small loan, say a few thousand pounds, then there are very few banks that are going to give much personal attention to your case.

You will merely form part of the process.

There will be letters. There may be calls. There will definitely be penalty charges added to your account.

Most banks have some form of "collect out department", a team of debt collectors essentially, that will chase you for your money. They may have the ability to negotiate repayment plans but, at the end of the day, you are part of the process and "just another account".

Don't take it personally. It's just a fact.

> *"And that's what I didn't understand. That [closing the account on liquidation] was so*

> *simple from the bank's side of view...that that could be actually done.*
>
> *And...erm...that they didn't seem to ... they didn't seem to care. That was the other side of it too. That there was no kind of like 'Oh, I'm awfully sorry about that' where it was kind of all matter of fact. 'Oh, that was just my life just disappeared there' and it was all just ticked away."*

So what should you do?

ACTION POINT 5.1 – Treat the bank like a supplier

How would you deal with any other supplier that is owed money?

The ideal is to owe them nothing (or, in this case, be within the terms of your facility).

But, failing that, pay as much off as you can.

If you are incurring charges due to the breach, compare those costs to any penalties being imposed by other creditors (they have the right to charge interest on any overdue debts). You can justify paying off one creditor ahead of another if there is good reason to do so.

Consequently, you should focus on repaying any debts with the largest penalties (to save on further costs).

It'll be a juggling exercise, but as long as you keep some things flowing, then you are likely to get a sensible response.

Don't forget, like any other supplier, you have the ability to find someone else that might give you better terms.

If, on the other hand, you have a large bank loan with a debenture over your company, and they are the main creditor of your company, things will be slightly different.

Say "Goodbye" to your bank manager?

You know that relationship manager that you have at your bank? The guy that is your best friend and will do anything you ask, as long as you promise to continue banking there. Well, you can say goodbye to them for now.

Most major banks have a separate function, an intensive care unit, within their organisation that is brought into play when your numbers start to head south. Most are called something like Business Support and someone from this team becomes your new relationship manager.

> *"The other thing that happens is that the bank move you away from your relationship people. So the people who know and trust you and that you can speak to, all that gets removed due to their bank processes."*

The timing of this and the level to which they get involved varies from bank to bank and, of course, the individual involved. We are going to have to be quite general in this chapter as we can't cover every situation, but you need to deal with the person that you find yourself with, regardless of the organisation.

> *"It's the guy you're sat in front of, not the bank."*

They're on my side. Aren't they?

How much is any supplier on your side?

> *"You get moved to somebody who's never met you before who clearly has worked with the accountants for many many years and clearly has a very close relationship with them. So you start to feel as if this is all a bit of a stitch up."*

Ultimately, their behaviour is determined by what their drivers are and the new manager has different priorities to the previous one.

Standard relationship managers are rewarded on income. The longer you stay as a client and the more services you use, the better off they are. So their interest is to keep you happy and to make you feel special.

Those from the intensive care unit have different motivations. Their job is to protect the bank's investment.

Their first preference is to help you to return to profitability and hand you back to your previous contact. I want to be very clear on this point, because it is worth bearing in mind. It means that you will get a lot of people who are incredibly supportive and understanding.

But, if things do continue to deteriorate, they will look at a re-finance, a sale of the business or, if things get really drastic, insolvency.

This means that, whilst they should be totally professional and courteous to you, you may not get the same level of "warmth" that you will have been used to and decisions made may appear to have been made contrary to your best interests.

Don't get me wrong, they don't want your company to go bust any more than you do, but the downside for them is not as high as it would be for your previous relationship manager.

Different banks have different triggers that will move you into their care unit but, once in, you will remain there until they are satisfied you are healthy enough to return to your normal status.

One thing that is very likely to happen is that they will appoint a firm of accountants to review your forecasts and figures.

> *"And they said 'Before we renew the facility, can we do a review of your affairs? And we'd*

> *like to appoint a firm of accountants to review where you are. There isn't a problem. They're just going to come in and just make sure that we're tickety-boo'.*
>
> *We were quite excited at the idea. 'They must know absolutely stacks about business and must be in a fantastic position to help us prepare for what's going forward. So fantastic.' So, I remember speaking to the bank and I think they were surprised. And I think that started to alarm me."*

The actual engagement letter will be between you and the accountants and it will be you that pays their fee. Now, this might lead you to think that they are working for you, with your best interests at heart.

> *"They were appointed by the business, not by the bank. So we very much saw that as being 'You're on our side and you're going to come in and give us advice as to how we can strengthen this business and keep the bank on board and take us through what is clearly starting to turn into a big storm.'*
>
> *And I think we were completely hoodwinked."*

However, when you get a copy of the report, you may find that not all is at it seems.

> *"The first time that I started to get worried was*

> *in December where a report was produced where we noticed that the bit we saw started at Chapter 4. And you think 'What ... what was Chapter 1,2 and 3?' And then there was another chapter missing. And then when we enquired they were like 'Well that's the bit that only the bank see.'*
>
> *But we paid the initial fee to them, it came out of my current account. So, that was the first time that we were thinking 'So you are now reporting to the bank secretly, and we're not privy to what that is.'*
>
> *And it was only when we flagged that, that the attitude started to shift.*
>
> *We were quickly called into the bank and told that they were stakeholders and that, in effect, that our shareholders' funds had gone and that they were ... that everything was now going to take a slightly different role."*

And when the bank calls you in for a meeting with the accountants present, it may not be clear where the relationships sit.

> *"So we never had an opportunity, really, to speak direct to the bank. The accountants would always go into the meeting first, we were then brought into the meeting with the bank. We were led down a series of questions and*

> *answers. We would then leave and the accountants would stay with the bank."*

Should the worst occur and your company go into administration, then you will find that the same firm of accountants will be appointed as administrators, where they will earn an even larger fee than the one that you paid them before the insolvency.

> *"We didn't realise that the company could appoint an advisor and the bank can appoint the same advisor to switch sides and start acting for the bank. I didn't think that was legal, to be perfectly honest, I thought that wasn't possible. I thought that whatever we told the accountants, 'cos they were company appointed, they were definitely acting on the behalf of the director and shareholder. So it came as a bit of a shock to me to suddenly see "Well, without you knowing we've switched sides. We're now working against you and everything you've told us can be used and we're also not allowing you to speak to the bank'."*

Which might lead you to question their objectivity in the first place.

> *"I don't want the bank to lose money. I felt as though the bank had offered me support and I thought they'd been very open and honest and honourable. And I didn't want them to lose a bean. And I was sending signals to the*

accountants, and openly saying to them, 'I am prepared to run the overheads of the business on my personal basis. I will pay them. In return for working for the bank to get the best return I can.'

I don't think that message was ever conveyed to the bank, from what I understand. 'Cos it wasn't in the accountants' interest to do that. They wanted the fees. Bluntly."

Oh, and by the way, you may well be charged higher bank fees to cover the cost of the extra support that you are getting?

How can the banks do that?

If you signed a loan agreement with your bank, you will probably have given security against that loan. Usually a debenture. Sometimes specific charges against particular assets. In some cases, you may even have given a personal guarantee with your house as backing.

"So?" You'll say. "That's what you do when you borrow money."

True, but like a mortgage over a house, the import of that document only sinks in when you fail to keep up those damn payments and the bailiff is knocking on the door.

Naturally, the bank is not going to leap straight

towards any form of possession without looking at other avenues first. Commercially it wouldn't make sense.

But within your facility agreement, there will be clauses that allow the bank to pretty much do as they please, particularly if you breach any of your pre-agreed covenants.

They have the power to, among other things:

- change the interest rate you pay and increase your bank charges;

- instruct a firm of accountants to come in and review your books, processes and forecasts. The report will often contain sections that only the bank sees and yet you will be made to pay for its production;

- request that any free assets be brought into their sphere of legal control in exchange for continued support;

- require changes to the board, including the appointment of a specialist turnaround director;

- demand instant re-payment of their loan. Failure to do so will result in them placing the company into administration.

As long as they have a debenture in place, they "own" your company.

And the balance of power has now shifted. You now need them more than they need you, so playing the valued customer card is not going to work.

Now, if you are reading this thinking that this can't happen to you. That you have a great relationship with your bank having been a valued customer for many years. Time to think again.

> *"We noticed that the bank were keeping all the receipts from any sales. So you make a sale and we'd put it in our cashflow. The money would be grabbed by the bank, so it would never enter the account and then they would ring you up to say we'd gone overdrawn.*
>
> *Well, you've grabbed the money, so what can we do?"*

At the end of the day banks are running a business. Like any business they have a responsibility to their shareholders and when there is a bad debt, it needs paying.

Whoever your bank contact is, they will have someone more senior to them giving instructions and they will be looking at numbers and following a process. And it won't matter what your track record is or how long you've been a customer, the bank will treat you as just another account that needs paying.

What can I do about it?

Before we progress any further, it is imperative that we establish one thing. Where are you on your personal curve right now?

In other words, if it hasn't done so already, now is the time for the penny to drop. If the bank is worried about your long term future, then you most definitely need to be as well.

And be sure that you are fully prepared to battle for your company. If the earlier exercises made you question whether you ought to be still doing what you're doing, now would be a good time to start discussing exit plans.

The next few months will need all of your resolve, emotional energy and discipline. You need to be fully motivated to make sure you succeed.

ACTION POINT 5.2 - Stay in control of your emotions

This is the really tough part, but how you conduct yourself in your discussions with your new bank manager is critical.

You may feel insulted, threatened or just badly treated by the bank for them dealing with you in such a manner. After all the years of working together, they come down on you like a ton of bricks at the first hint of a wobble. After all, this is just an unfortunate dip, not the start of a slide.

You may feel that a huge amount of trust with the bank has been lost.

These are normal reactions to what can be quite a dramatic change in circumstances.

But don't act up on those feelings.

In the same way that waving your arms around when a wasp is nearby is more likely to get you stung, so an aggressive response to the bank will only make things worse.

Your quickest route out is to be helpful, open, polite, understanding and prepared to make any changes the bank wants to see.

You might be hurting inside initially but in the long run you'll be better off.

ACTION POINT 5.3 - Stay in control of your business

One of the easiest things to do when the banks and the accountants start to get involved is to let other things in your business slip. This is likely to lead to more investigations and more reports and closer levels of monitoring, until you suddenly realise that you are no longer in real control of your own company.

Also, be aware that the banks and the accountants will go to great lengths to make sure that they can't be treated as shadow directors of your company. That means that you won't get any specific or direct advice, and yet, somehow, you end up not having a choice.

> *"We were expecting far more guidance from the accountants and the bank than we got. In fact we got no guidance from either. We would often have hypothetical discussion with them, and say, 'Hypothetically, you could do this and hypothetically you could do that'."*

Dealing with the bank

The best result for you is for the bank to hand you back to your original relationship manager as quickly as possible.

To do this, you first must understand precisely the reasons for you being in the specialist support section of the bank and what you need to do to get out. If you are not sure of something, then make sure you ask the question up front.

You must then work **with** the bank, not against them. The more you take a head on resistance approach to the problem, the more likely you are to get squashed.

We've talked before about picking your battles and making the right choices. Similarly, by spending all of your energies on fighting the bank, you spend less time on sorting out the issues and the proper running of your business. Very quickly you can lose control.

Take a more subtle approach.

Run with the bank. When they ask for information, get them that information. If they suggest changes, make the changes. If you promise them something, deliver on that promise. On time.

Now, I must stress, that this doesn't mean becoming the bank's whipping boy.

It is important that you demonstrate that you are a good leader and an expert in your field. If you think something is wrong, then say so. But in an open and collaborative spirit rather than a dismissive, confrontational manner.

If you are prepared to make changes and accept new things, you will find that you may actually benefit from the situation.

Job interview

Imagine that your new bank contact is interviewing you for your job. Don't presume that they have any prior knowledge of your strengths. It is for you to demonstrate, in these next few weeks, that you are competent and deserving of being in control.

By working with the bank and showing them how competent you are, they will come to trust and respect you. This will lead to a greater level of support going forward and less attention required by the bank (which will also keep costs down).

This, in turns, mean that you stay in control. Then, by being in the driving seat, you have a greater influence on direction.

So, dealing with the bank's key issues will be your top priority over the next few weeks, but you need to balance that with the ongoing demands of the business.

Once you have the facts to hand, you need to hold a proper planning session to schedule what needs to be done in the short term. Take into account what changes may be needed to the business, what specific information needs to be given to the bank and how long that will take and, of course, what needs to be done to keep your business moving along.

You then need to allocate roles and responsibilities to your team or, if it's just you, start prioritising really quickly.

Dealing with the accountants

The unwanted intrusion of an unknown firm, looking under the furniture and criticising the decor, can be another moment of tension and frustration for directors.

However, we once again have a situation where there is little you can do to stop it and the more you resist, the more difficult it will be to move forward.

Furthermore, the banks take the advice of the accountants very seriously. The opinions, both formal and informal, that the accountants pass on to the banks, could have a serious impact on your future.

This means that you now have a good opportunity to get your main points across.

The accountants will be on site, getting deep into the business. If you are able to convince them of your strengths and the company's future, then this will be relayed back and may influence the opinion of the bank.

You should therefore treat this period as a time to be at your best.

Now, unless you have a fixed fee agreement in place, their costs are likely to be based on an hourly rate. Irrespective of what caps and discounted rates you may be able to negotiate, the long and the short of it is that the less work they need to do, the less it will cost.

The process is likely to run something along the following lines:

- Initial meeting and discussion;
- Request for certain information;
- Questions regarding the information;
- Request for additional information;
- Draft report provided for accuracy of information;
- Final report.

That may seem quite simple, but there will be a lot of information needed and a lot of questions asked.

Your task is to make sure that they are given full access to you, your team and the information and to ensure that the process runs as smoothly as possible. This will minimise the time they need to spend on the project.

If you can, depending on the size of your business, allocate a fairly senior individual to be the main point of contact for the accountants.

Whether that be you, the FD or the financial controller doesn't matter too much, but by having a focal point that can co-ordinate the distribution of information and answers to questions, the disruption to the rest of your business will be minimised and any competing demands can be appropriately prioritised.

> *"Every day there was something else. Questions from the accountants and customers and one thing or another. Like every single day. Looking back it was quite stressful."*

However, you need to properly allocate this person to the role, rather than having them squeeze in these extra demands in with their day job. Be prepared for them to be fully occupied for a good few days, maybe longer.

Their top priority should be to assist the accountants: providing information requested as quickly as possible and in a user friendly or the requested format; responding to questions promptly and accurately; providing access to other team members that the accountants wish to meet etc.

It is better to lose the work of one person for a few days than the disruption that can be caused by several people trying to do several things at once and without overall cohesion.

> *"We were being run ragged by the accountants doing lots of reports in lots of areas. So we were running cashflow after cashflow after cashflow. The FD and I were working massive hours, just producing documents. We weren't able to run the business because we were just producing documents for the bank and the accountants which we gave absolute priority to."*

By working with them, not only will the accountant's onsite presence be kept to a minimum, it also portrays a professional and efficient image that you can be sure will be reported back to the bank.

If you don't believe that you can spare an individual for this role, then how would you cope when they go on holiday or if they were to fall ill?

> *"You can go choose to go one of two ways. You can spend the next year or eighteen months fighting with the accountants and the banks and you will probably survive another year or eighteen months, but you will die. Or you work with them, you be very open with them, be very honest with them and, you may still die, but [if you do] you will die a fairly..er.. almost painless death with them and you will get through it fairly quickly and then you have an opportunity to come back quickly."*

ACTION POINT 5.4 - Listen to advice

Even though you may think that the new bank manager and the accountants don't know your business and have no right to make suggestions as to how you improve things, just take a moment to think about it.

These people are experts at looking at ways on how to save money, increase profits and rescue businesses.

Surely there must be something you can learn from them?

If you are concerned that they don't know your business, then it is your job to make sure that they do. Give them the information they need, talk to them, explain everything and give them no excuse for not understanding what you are attempting to do, how you are going about it and why you are doing it in that way.

Now, if you are feeling protective about your business or scared that they are going to criticise your methods: or indeed, believe that your business is already perfect and needs no improvement, then take pause for a moment.

Nothing is ever perfect. Everything can be improved.

If you have to sacrifice a bit of pride in order to get some suggestions that will help your business become more successful and you richer, isn't that a price worth paying?

ACTION POINT 5.5 – Stay in control of the relationship

If you follow the previous action points then you should be building and maintaining trust with the accountants and the bank, which is where you need to be if you want them to do you any favours.

Now it becomes important that you start to shift the power balance a little bit back to you. Not in a sneaky underhand way, but by working with the trust and respect that you have earned to date. Here are some suggestions in this respect.

Be proactive

If the bank has commissioned a report from the accountants, what often happens is that the accountants come in to do their field work, go off to write a report, send a draft to the bank, wait for them to read the highlights and then, finally, give you an opportunity to discuss the results with them. And this can take several weeks.

A common mistake that directors make is to hold off making any improvements or changes to their business, waiting to hear what the accountants and the banks have to say.

> *"And I think we were wanting to say 'What do you want us to do? If you want us to get rid of everybody and put it down to four/five staff, then we can, but the repercussions of that: I can't possibly hit your target. I can't possibly do the growth that I've talked about and I can't possibly honour some of the commitments that we've got.' So we were almost in limbo.*
>
> *And we thought at the end of this big report, that we were told was coming from the*

accountants that there would be a battle plan with the bank on board and us on board, as to how we were going to solve the problem.

So we're sat waiting for this report which we thought would involve £5 million pounds of active money still coming through the system, which of course was lost when we went into administration."

Remember, it is your business. If you spot things that will reduce costs and increase cash, you don't need permission to go ahead and do it.

By delaying several weeks you may miss an opportunity or waste money, so you may as well got on with things.

Treat the Intensive Care Unit as a customer

"We weren't looking at what the bank was asking for."

We talked before about the bank being a supplier.

Previously, whilst your cash flow was strong, the lending fully secured and you stayed within your limits and covenants, you controlled the relationship and the bank **was** just another supplier to your company. You had the power to move your facility elsewhere and deny them the benefit of your custom.

Now, that ability to move is not quite so easy. Either other banks won't lend to you as there isn't enough security around to make the deal sufficiently low risk, or you need to pay through the nose for some form of specialised funding.

This means that the relationship is now controlled by the bank, not you.

In effect, they have now become your most important customer and you must supply them with what they want and when they want it, or it could seriously damage your business.

Specifically, your new relationship manager from the intensive care unit.

As a general rule, we tend to be more amenable to our customers than our suppliers. We need to win and keep our customers, meaning that they need to be kept supplied and satisfied. Consequently, when they become demanding, we tend to be more understanding and forgiving, often bending over backwards to fulfil a difficult order at short notice rather than let them down.

By adjusting your focus and thinking of the intensive care unit of the bank as an important customer, so the psychological approach will change. The levels of animosity and conflict should reduce and a more collaborative and positive environment can be achieved.

In this state, the ability to benefit from the bank's experience and flourish as a business is greatly enhanced.

Give them the bad news

Counter-intuitive? Not at all. As mentioned above, it's all about trust. If you have skeletons in the closet, they will be discovered eventually.

How much better it is to pull problems out early and deal with them together, than to try and bury things and look like you were trying to get away with it.

Banks do not like surprises.

By owning up to issues yourself and early on, you will be respected and trusted to do the right thing and the bank will reduce the pressure on you. Remember about retaining control.

So:

- don't fiddle the forecasts to make them look better than they could ever hope to be. This will only cause greater problems further down the line;

- don't hide that piece of bad news that's cropped up (say, the loss of a major contract), and hope nobody will notice. They will - and they won't thank you for keeping it quiet; and

- never defend the indefensible. Take a proper look at your business. Applaud and support the good elements, by all means, but very few things are perfect, so recognise how things could be better.

Remember, the banks are not looking to blame you or criticise you. All they want is to make your business work better. Which, hopefully, you do too.

If you don't acknowledge the hidden issues, they don't get dealt with quickly. If they don't get dealt with quickly, they may end up becoming too big to resolve.

Engage independent help

When the banks have appointed their own advisors, there is nothing to stop you getting advice from someone else.

Not to repeat the work of the bank's accountants. That would be a waste of time and money. But someone that knows the banks and the other accountants and is on your side. That way you will have a better insight into how the bank thinks and what they might be looking for, allowing you to anticipate their next move and maintain that pro-activity.

However, don't just appoint a main rival to the other accountants. You want to be seen to be getting advice but not challenging the banks or their advisors.

Plus it can bring into question the motivation of your own advisors.

> *"He was so excited about the prospect himself, he tried to get me to appoint him on the very final day. So there was a little bit of argy bargy on the day I put it into administration as to whether I had the right to appoint my choice of accountant or the bank's choice of accountant, which was my right. And there was a bit of fall out on the day because my accountants were saying 'Seeing as it is such a juicy case, we think there's well over a million pounds of fees in this. We would really like it.'*
>
> *The professional team then is quite, the supportive team is fantastic. Again, you realise why it's fantastic, because they're all getting bloody fees. So nobody could do enough for us.*
>
> *So our accountants took us in and give you lunch. They couldn't do enough for us. And that's when they said 'Well can ... please can you appoint ... you know, after you've eaten your chicken sandwich can we be appointed please, because there's a million pounds at stake here?'*
>
> *So you do start to feel as if you're being fed to the vultures."*

I would remind you of one of the points raised way back in Chapter 1. If you want personal support, that support needs to come from someone independent of the decision you make regarding the business.

> *"I think through all of this that you realise how selfish companies are 'cos they look after their own interests. At no point did anyone look at me or look at how I interacted with everything else."*

I should emphasise here that we have been discussing the worst case situations where the companies in question have **not** been proactive and have **not** acted when they should.

At no point should you ever take away the impression that you are making a mistake in seeking business advice from a professional.

The earlier you seek help, the better it will be all round. Turnaround and restructuring professionals engaged by you prior to the banks getting involved will be working much more for your benefit, meaning that the issues raised in this chapter are less likely to arise.

However, the longer you delay taking action, the more likely you are to hand control of the decision making process over to others, and the more complicated the situation will become.

ACTION POINT 5.6 - Plan for the worst

For all the efforts you've made to work with the bank and the accountants, remember that they are not actually on your side. That doesn't mean to say they are against you, either. They are on their own side and, whilst you run in parallel with them, all is fine. But as soon as the bank's agenda moves, you are in trouble.

> *"We also, looking back, made ourselves extremely vulnerable to go down because there wasn't much ... when the accountants were finally appointed as administrators, there wasn't much work in progress. So we put ourselves beautifully into, from the bank's perspective, into a stop position. So they didn't need us. So I would say that we were doing it by the rule book, which is when things are tough, get rid of your day to day production staff. Stop producing because you're not selling at the same rate. But that does play beautifully into the hands of your lender."*

You have a very fine balance to hold between being open and honest and co-operating fully with the bank and the accountants, without actually trusting either.

> *"But you realise now that a lot of the people advising you have their eyes on their own business, which is 'How can I bring fees in too?'*

> *The lawyers or the accountants, whatever, they've got their own profit lines. They're not necessarily there as your friend to help you get through a difficult time. Which is hard to get in your head."*

You need to look at all possible scenarios, including a possible insolvency, and plan accordingly.

> *"Don't spend 100% of your time trying to save that one limited company. You've got to spend a proportion of your time thinking of yourself and your wellbeing and you've got to spend a portion of your time thinking what you can do in the future if this limited company goes down against your will, if you like.*
>
> *Don't spend all your time convinced ... it's a bit like being on the Titanic. Don't spend all your time convinced that you can bloody avoid that iceberg. Spend **a lot** of time trying to avoid the iceberg but also spend a lot of time thinking 'I might end up in a lifeboat and I might have to bloody swim for it.'*
>
> *So, think about it and start working out how that would physically work. And it's really difficult.*
>
> *And I've had many a director sat in front of me, who's on the edge of mental issues basically, because mentally it is destroying them. That*

the bank is not giving them answers, not giving them support. Their advisors are not supporting them. And it comes as a massive shock to them when I say:

'They won't! They will not.

And you are on your own. And you are way out of your depth and you are on your own in the deep sea and **you** *need to work out how you're going to survive. And it might mean that you have to bust the firm.'"*

Summary

The relationship with your bank is a difficult one.

You have got used to them being, effectively, your business partner and have been given promises of help and support. Suddenly, it's all changed and those promises appear to stand for nothing.

For you to get back on track the most critical thing that you can do is get real and deal with it.

Don't waste time putting up barriers and raging at their behaviour. You have their money, so you have to dance to their tune. The quicker you accept that fact, the sooner you will be left alone.

The bottom line is that they do want you to survive and do well and will only take strong action if you give them reason to think otherwise, and the longer that you are in the intensive care unit the more reasons you are giving them. So don't relax until you are out.

Until things are back to normal, always plan for the worse but act for the best.

So, we've now had a look at some of the things that could be causing you a problem. Financial downturns and bank attitudes can have a major impact on how your business performs.

However, these are merely factors, not necessarily causes. We have yet to deal with the biggest problem that you have to face. This we shall do in the next chapter.

CHAPTER 6 : THE BIGGEST PROBLEM

You may be the best business person in the country. You may have a business that has been around for years and has an excellent reputation for being successful. You may pride yourself on the efficiency of your organisation and the team spirit of your employees.

However, not everything is under your control.

When you are facing a massive change in your business life, either due to the changes enforced on you by the bank, the dawning realisation that the losses are not going to reverse this time or actually staring the spectre of insolvency in the face, it is extremely difficult to carry on performing at your best.

It doesn't matter who you are, when you are under stress, you behave differently. This is what happens when you move further down your personal curve towards the lowest point.

> *"When you're down there you sometimes think 'Fuck it, I've had enough! I'll just go and jump off a bridge'. And when you do get that low, you just don't want the telephone to ring. You sit in the house and you're terrified of a phone call, because it's always a problem. You can't relate to any phone that rings. You shit yourself. 'It's a*

> *problem! What shall I do?' And the alarm bells go off.*
>
> *You smile and stuff like that but all you want to do is get yourself in a cupboard with the doors locked."*

There will be very practical steps that you can take that make absolute logical sense and you won't take them.

> *"You get a lot of self talk. And when you're on a downer, you don't get much good advice, do you? It's all negative stuff. But then after that you think 'Ah give us another week and it'll turn the corner'."*

The biggest problem is not the situation you find yourself in.

The biggest problem is how you react to it.

> *"I didn't realise at the time that the biggest problem I had was actually not the liquidation and not the financial situation. The biggest problem I had at the time, was me."*

Of course, if you are the problem ... then you are also the solution.

Feeling helpless

> *"I'd done it for that long and I was quite good at it and all of a sudden it was out of my control."*

After years of being in charge of their own business and their own destiny, one of the hardest things for a director to comprehend is that they are not in control of everything.

When that control is taken away from them, a feeling of helplessness can arise.

> *"And you go home and you're thinking ... you're looking at your lass and you're thinking 'bloody hell.'*
>
> *You're talking. You're not listening to what they're saying. You're talking but you're not listening 'cos your mind's elsewhere."*

When the natural tendency is to find control again, it can lead to desperate grabs for any control that they can find. Very often this leads to fighting forlornly against immovable barriers or raging against the smallest of things.

> *"I didn't know how to calm myself down. So I was like ready to fire off at anything. This woman came into the shop ... and I couldn't help it ... stressed as hell, you know what I mean ... and she starts questioning prices. She carries on questioning prices ... and she were the landlady! ... she had every right to do it ... and I just sort of flipped. I said 'Look, if you're not happy, you can fuck off!'*
>
> *And then I thought 'Damn it, you knob head.*

> *Why did you say that?' I couldn't help it, you know what I mean? Because it was like she were havin' a slate at me."*

Decision making

When you lose focus on what you want to achieve and feel like you've lost control of the situation, the thought of making any form of decision can be quite daunting.

> *"I shied away from some decisions. One of which should have been to probably sit down with my wife and go 'Listen. I'm going to be open and honest with you. I can't do this anymore. I know you probably think we've not given it enough time but: a); b); c) ... whatever.'*
>
> *We talked about what was my decision making like ... Poor! I avoided the important decisions because I just wanted to ... to kind of not make a decision really. I wanted time to make the decision for me or somebody else to make the decision for me."*

Or, when you do make a decision, it ends up being the wrong one.

> *"You tend not to make decisions that are too big. You put them away until you feel a bit better.*
>
> *Oh, probably, yeah. When I went to*

> *conferences, I bought too much stock.*
>
> *'Cos I ran away with the whole thing. Ended coming back with 40 bloody items outside the shop and all on my own.*
>
> *'Everything gonna be all right. Don't worry about it. Get it. You gotta buy this, you gotta buy that. You gotta buy four of them, four of them, four of them.'*
>
> *Then it's 'Damn! I've got to pay for that bastard. Shit!' Lots of stock, no money."*

Without some form of external support, it can be extremely difficult to have any objective clarity on what you need to do.

Fatigue

By fatigue, I don't mean just being physically tired. That will be a consequence of the lack of sleep. I'm talking about the lack of that deep rooted emotional energy.

In some cases, this may be because you're actually not enjoying what you do.

> *"My perception of help back then was, well two things really. I couldn't afford any, if I needed it. Or I thought I couldn't afford any. But also I think deep down I knew that the business was flawed. My heart wasn't in it anyway."*

Which can often be a consequence of a flawed business.

> *"One of the things I hadn't made allowances for was the team of people who worked for me. 'Cos they basically weren't good enough and it was coming out. And so I was learning a lot about myself as well and what I needed to do. It was basically just a clusterfuck as I didn't have the right people. I didn't have enough good customers and the market was shifting incredibly fast. So basically it was a no-brainer. It was going to go."*

However, the most common reason is that your brain never switches off.

> *"It's knowing how to relax. It's knowing how to relax that [points to head].*
>
> *It's the key to everything. If you can't relax that ... it's racing and racing and racing. It's like a long distance runner, isn't it? Suddenly it's got to stop for a drink. And then, once you've stopped running, when you've run like three marathons on the trot, it's hard to get them legs going again, isn't it? 'Cos you've hit that wall. And I think that's your problem when your mind's whirring all the time. It just needs to jog a bit.*
>
> *It's good to run, but it's nice to jog sometimes.*

> *Or even walk. Not sprint about everywhere in your head."*

Lack of trust

When you're under pressure and in a situation that you have never faced before, it can be a very difficult to place your trust in anyone else.

> *"My motto in life has been 'There is only one person I believe in in this world and that's me.' You know, I've always just believed in myself, in what I'm doing. Believed in what I'm doing is right. Believed in what I'm doing is okay. And that's it. And I've always been in that frame of mind. If you don't believe in anybody else, believe in yourself. Because there is only you, at the end of the day, to rely on."*

And it is easy to find examples where trust is in short supply.

> *"People aren't as honest as I thought they were. I mean, a councillor ... to us he was an upright citizen representing our council. He was part of the town. And there he was, he had a lease from the council and he was actually trading illegally to our detriment. And I just thought 'How pathetic can you get?' And I just didn't think that things happened like that."*

In addition to trusting the motivations of others, there can be concerns that no-one else out there can possibly understand what you're going through.

> *"You can't really talk to a lot of people about it, 'cos unless they've actually been in there with it, they're not going to understand what you're talking about."*

Worried about what others think

> *"Why didn't I listen? Pride more than anything."*

Good old pride. Where would we be without it?

> *"You get all these people around you. And so their expectations of me were 'He's started his own business. He's the only one of the family or circle of friends to have done that. You're gonna be Alan Sugar.' And then it doesn't do that and what I've realised over the years is that each time I've done that and failed to go as far as I thought I could have done, it's chipped away at my own self esteem."*

And all internally generated.

> *"I think a small part of it is my perception of their expectation. 'Cos I don't think anybody ever sort of ... you know ... said anything out loud about what their expectations of me are."*

There are also concerns about how it impacts on other people over and above your own health.

> *"You think you'll let people down, don't you? You just worry every day. Some days you're doing 7 days a week 'cos you can't afford to pay people. I'd be talking to you now and the words would be coming out, but I wouldn't be listening. I'd just be ... I'd be somewhere else. I'd still be talking but I would not listen, I know that. It messes you up big style. You can't sleep ... well you can sleep because sometimes you feel that depressed you just want to go to bed. You know what I mean. So sometimes you have good days and you have bad days."*

It is very easy to let the concerns of others drag you down.

> *"The factors that reduce your courage are: the potential shame ... perceived shame actually; the letting down of people that you care about. That's at the real heart of it. And that's from the immediate flesh and blood: the children who're probably actually mostly unaware of the real extent of what's happening; your partner and your parents if they're involved; and then the people that were connected to us either because they'd invested with us or just our friends who cared about us - and the feeling of letting them down.*
>
> *The feeling of ... 'cos everyone has them in life. Those people who said 'It won't work' or 'You're no good at that.' or, you know, 'What have you*

> *ever done?' the seeming ... the perception that all that has been validated and it's true.*
>
> *You're probably in a very fragile state at that point and my reaction, basically, was to go into my cave. I just didn't really engage. I didn't go out socially and I definitely, for probably I reckon a good 6 months, maybe 9 months, prior to the final collapse. I just stopped being sociable entirely.*
>
> *And I realise now that it was a reflection of my low self esteem and the idea of being in a networking environment where I might have actually encountered somebody who knew what had gone wrong was the worst thing in the world."*

Letting go

> *"Agony. Didn't want to let go. I think that's the hardest thing. Letting go. You've spent so long building something up and always ... it was agonising seeing things not work out the way you want."*

Whether it's a group of people, a division of the company or the business itself. Giving up on something that feels like part of you is tough. No wonder people delay in taking action.

> *"And that's the thing, yeah. Letting go. Letting go of things quicker and not dragging them out.*

> *Realising when something has just got to the end of its life."*

Emotionally, you have to find the right time for you.

> *"As an individual, you know you're ready. When you hit that lowest ... I think it's the same as being an alcoholic. When it hits you, you know you're ready, and then you need somebody to talk to."*

ACTION POINT 6.1 – Give your brain some cooling off time

What sort of things are you thinking about on a daily basis? What are the topics that your conscious mind cogitates over?

Feel free to list out the things you think of (broad-brush categories); put them in a pie chart format or just reflect. Whatever works for you.

Don't forget to have a look at the exercise where you listed out the things that were most important to you, if you need inspiration.

How much of your waking time is spent thinking about your business and worrying about how it impacts on everything else?

If the majority of your waking hours are spent constantly fretting over what is going on, then you need to introduce something new or else you are going to burn out. Go and play some sport. Go to the gym. Take up yoga or meditation. Help out for a local charity. Join a choir.

Just do something that makes you concentrate on something else for an hour or so.

By doing that you give your brain a chance to recover, so that it can be more effective when dealing with some difficult decision.

ACTION POINT 6.2 – Find out what's stopping you

For this exercise, keep in mind what you've worked on before. Things that are important to you and the elements of your current role that you are fighting for.

What's the worst that could happen?

Now, write down every possible outcome that you can think of for your business. I'll give you most of them here:

- Business turns around and flourishes;
- Business is sold to a third party in roughly current format;
- Parts of business are closed down to allow the remainder to survive;
- Business goes through an insolvency and you buy some or all of it back;

- Business goes through an insolvency and is sold to a third party;
- Business goes through an insolvency and is shut down.

If you can think of any other options, then add them to the list, but in broad terms, these are the main options out there.

Have a look at the options and circle two of them.

One that is your absolute favourite and preferred option. And one that, if Option 1 were not available, that you would settle for.

Second favourite

Get some blank paper and, at the top of the first page, write down that SECOND option as a header.

On the page below the header, write down/mind-map everything that needs to happen for that outcome to be achieved.

Not just one or two things. Everything you can think of.

And no editing. If you don't like the look of something or it seems impossible, still include it. In fact, it's vital that these ones are included.

Don't stop there

And then, for everything that you've written down, ask yourself what needs to happen for that to be achieved and add to the list or mind map even further.

As soon as one avenue gets to a point where, although more work is required to fine tune it, you know it is an area that you are comfortable with and roughly what to do. Stop. Save that route for later.

Concentrate on the difficult routes and the unpopular choices. The areas of uncertainty and doubt.

You may have to make some assumptions but think practically about what would have to happen, however horrible, for it to take place. And see where that route takes you.

Every route should end up with an action that you are required to do in order for it to progress. If it ends up with an action required to be done by somebody else, then you need to ask them to do it, so that is an action for you.

Every avenue will then end up, either in an area that you are happy that it can be achieved, or that you think is impossible.

Is it really impossible?

Make sure you are clear about whether the 'impossible' action is:

- something that **you** can't do;
- something you aren't willing to do; or
- it is an absolute universal law that it will never happen.

If the action required lies within either of the first two categories, be aware that whether you do it or not is actually a choice on your part and only something that you can decide.

Review your options

Now, regardless of how much you desire the outcome at the top of the page, what is actually stopping you from doing it?

If the actions required are so difficult or so repugnant that you can never contemplate taking the steps required, then cross out that outcome.

Yes. That's right. Cross the entire outcome off the list.

And that's fine. That is something you have control over. That is something you either decided to do or is fundamentally impossible to achieve. That is an outcome you now no longer need to worry about.

If the thought of crossing that outcome out doesn't fit right with you, then you need to re-explore what needs to be done. What do you need to do to keep that option alive?

And, if all of the steps are do-able, then you have an action plan. If need be, you can get on and do it.

But ...

That was your second favourite outcome. There are other outcomes available.

Other outcomes

You will probably find that your favourite option will take longer to work through, so be aware. Ultimately, it would be good to do a similar exercise for every single one of the options that you have listed.

It is best not to do it all in one go, but spend some time every day working on a different one.

And, as you go through, cross off any outcomes that you are confident that you are not able to achieve.

Not whether you <u>want</u> to achieve it or not. The one you want the least is probably the easiest to achieve (i.e. do nothing at all and it will go bust). So don't cross that outcome off the list.

"We always thought there was going to be support and rescue. We never thought there would be administration. And we drew up lots of plans for how that [rescue] would work and we were constantly doing cashflows and analysis and presenting to the bank on how that would work. And we always believed, almost right up until the last day.

So we were a bit shocked then, when we came to a meeting where we were going for a regular update meeting. And we thought we'd gone in with some fairly positive news. We were operating within the agreed overdraft facilities, we were paying massive chunks of interest. And the representative from the bank said 'I'm sorry. This is not the meeting you're expecting. We are unable to offer you any kind of facilities and we can't do anything for you further. Full stop'."

Do what is within your control

The key thing with this exercise is that we cannot choose the outcomes themselves. All we can do is choose the actions that we take. If that increases the chances of a certain outcome occurring, then that is what we do. Because that is where we have control.

Don't pursue an outcome you want if you are not prepared or able to take the steps needed for that outcome to be achieved.

Alternatively, if keeping the outcome as a possible reality is so important to you, then you will find the strength you need to overcome the barriers that you have placed in front of yourself.

> *"Be more realistic. Do what has to be done. Say what has to be said. I'm tougher than I used to be. Do what has to be done for the best, even if it makes you uncomfortable."*

If you are the problem, then you are the solution.

> *"It's up to me to decide how big a problem 'the company going bust' is. If you get back on your feet and you make millions of pounds inside of two years, how big a problem **was** that? It was a hiccup.*
>
> *If this is the end of your life as you know it and you live a miserable life thereafter. Yes, it was a big problem.*
>
> *So you decide the size or the extent of the problem."*

Summary

It isn't what happens to you which is the problem. It is how you handle it.

It is very easy to get caught up in the emotion and the fear of everything, which leads to panic and stress and, in turn, poor decision making and possible health issues.

If you can gain control of yourself then, whatever happens to the business, you will be in a good position going forward.

So, give your brain a chance to relax and then spend some time really thinking about what lies within your control. Then you can take action.

If you are still feeling scared about taking some of these difficult actions, then the next chapter may help you to overcome some of those feelings.

CHAPTER 7 : FEAR IS THE MINDKILLER

> *"I'm terrified of finding out the accounts now. I think that's locked in because of the failed business. I'm terrified about going to the bank and finding out how much money I've got in. Because for me to phone up a bank or talk to a bank is rejection. Scared of them saying 'You haven't got enough sir.'*
>
> *I've checked today and I've got enough in, but to make that phone call it's 'Bloody hell' Heart going 'boof boof'. It's horrible. When I see a letter from VAT and stuff like that ... I daren't open it. All they want is for me to fill a form in. But I daren't open it. Daren't. Because I'm terrified of what's inside it. And that's just because of that period. It's fucked my head up."*

What is fear?

We mentioned before how evolution has brought us to a state where, left to our own devices, we tend to take action only when there is an actual physical threat. However, we continue to receive warnings of fear and alarm as we go along.

This is there to prepare us for when we do finally need to take action. However, because there are very few situations where we are genuinely under physical threat, we end up getting waves and waves of these feelings of fear, and they keep increasing until something changes.

To give us the best chance of survival, the bit of our brain that sends out the warning signals suspects the worst every time. It's like an extreme insurance policy. In the wild, if you got it wrong, you died, so it's worth being a little over cautious.

In any area of uncertainty, our brains continue to build up the worst picture they can come up with and set us up for the whole 'Fight or Flight' scenario. In other words, by upping the adrenaline, shutting down the digestive system, shortening the breath and tensing up the muscles, we are in the best possible state for engaging in physical combat or for a quick dash to safety.

And this automatic state of readiness includes altering the flow of blood to the brain. The only thing that the conscious brain needs to focus on is the fighting and the fleeing, so the body diverts more blood to the arms and legs to increase strength and stamina.

In other words, it is extremely difficult to generate a wide range of options and follow an educated selection process when we are scared and under stress.

This is the reason that quiz shows set time limits, increase the moody music and overuse the spotlight. And why, for those of us sat at home, they look like idiots for not being able to answer really easy questions.

When faced with a major problem, we get too close to it, stare at it too hard and for too long and find it very difficult to come up with a good solution.

And all for no reason.

> *"When I'm working with people, I find that everybody hits the fear threshold. And fear is illogical. And you can get through it by shifting the belief system."*

Expectation vs reality

Now, in the absence of an actual physical threat, fear is generated via the absence of facts and the existence of uncertainty.

When something is new, untested, untried and unfamiliar, there we are more likely to find doubt and concern and we are more likely to fear it due to our brain thinking the worst.

However, the more we know, the less we get consumed by blind panic and the more we can make rational decisions.

Everyone I spoke to found that the reality of insolvency was much less painful than the expectation. The really bad things that they experienced were created by their own minds and, whilst things were never actually pleasant, they were a walk in the park compared to how they had foreseen things.

> *"The decision to actually put it into liquidation, the humility of doing that, was unbelievable. Where you actually don't need to feel so humiliated. Because it's not such a bad thing if you do all in your power to prevent it happening.*
>
> *You know, there are things we could have done earlier, which may have prevented it. And you may be naïve, but if you do the best of your ability with that naivety then you shouldn't ... you shouldn't need to feel that humiliated. And all the pressure that comes with that. 'Cos it's a fact of life."*

In the previous chapter I encouraged you to look at every eventuality, including the business going through an insolvency. For many people, just the thought of it would be enough to cause their chest to tighten, their neck to constrict and to leave them feeling sick.

In this chapter, I want to bring some reality into the demise of a business.

This is not with a view to pushing people unnecessarily down that route but, if they can look at the situation for what it is and without the huge emotional response that is often associated with insolvency, then they will be better equipped to make a sensible decision, and without so much pain.

You are not your business

> *"You think of it as 'you'. That the business is an extension of 'you'. And it isn't. It's a limited company. And it isn't you and you mustn't get too attached to it because it stops you from doing what is necessary in the best interest of the business. Because you take it too personally. So I would say that that's a massive lesson that I've learnt."*

The words are obvious, but this is such a fundamental trap that we all fall into.

When we have been involved with the running of a business for a long time, especially if we were involved in setting it up in the first place, we invest so much emotional energy and personal identity into it that the line between where we end and the business starts becomes blurred.

> *"Should have liquidated it faster. Done it straight away. But I've got to give it a try. The problem I had was, it was my identity. I didn't have anything else."*

Every statement, action, failure and success of the business becomes a reflection of our own views and our own results.

Consequently, when the business fails, we fail. And when the business goes down, it can drag us with it.

> *"Especially from a mining background, 'cos you learn to work hard. If you want something, work hard.*
>
> *Play football, you want to get in the best side. Work hard. If you want to play golf, practice, work hard, work hard. That's how I've been brought up, you know what I mean? That's how a lot of us in South Yorkshire are.*
>
> *We see ... it's failure. If yer business don't work, it's failure. I've been taught all my life, it's working hard. Not working sensibly. Fuckin' hard."*

This is why it can take as much as two years for a director or business owner to recover from the downfall of their business. They don't see it as a venture that just happened not to work. They believe that it is a part of them. That it had died and cannot be resurrected.

But we are talking about a business. A set of systems created to generate money out of combining products, skills and time. Not a person or even part of a person.

> *"I'm certainly not attached to this business as I was to that. And if somebody wants to come along and buy me out, they can with pleasure. But you'd would never have taught me that prior to the bust. I had to learn that the bloody hard way."*

ACTION POINT 7.1 – What's important to your business?

So, fresh bit of paper needed and draw a line down the middle of it.

Spend some time thinking of all the things that are important **to your business**. As they come to you, write them on the left hand side.

Don't worry about order or level of importance. Just get them down.

Think about why the business does what it does. Who the business does it for. The way the business goes about doing things. Anything that you feel is important, put it on the list.

Keep going until you can't think of any more. Then write down another 3.

Prioritise

Okay. Now look at each entry on the list in turn and give them a mark out of 10 as to how important they are to the business, with 10 being essential.

Review the list and, if you have any items scoring 5 or lower, cross them out.

Once you've done that, transfer the list to the right hand side but, this time, in order of importance with the most important ones at the top. Where you have several entries with the same score, prioritise appropriately.

Time to review

You have listed out what is important to your business.

A few chapters back you did exactly the same thing in terms of what is important to you. If you didn't do it, go back and do that now. Otherwise, go and find that previous list and compare the two.

How similar are they?

There will be overlaps and similarities, naturally, because your ethics and values will be imposed on the business. But they will not be identical.

And they are not identical because you are not the same thing.

Consequently, one can exist without the other. It is entirely possible for the business to be sold to someone else or to go on existing in your absence.

Similarly, your wellbeing and existence is not conditional on that of your business.

Please remember this the next time that you are reviewing options for the business.

Whilst you're here, just spend some time looking at the differences between what's important to you and what's important to your business.

See if there is anything else you can learn from them. I'll leave that one with you.

The Gambler

The best way of looking at a business venture or a company is to think of it as a bet.

You are the gambler that has studied the form and invested an element of money on the outcome of an event.

You may have some influence on the outcome but there will always be elements outside of your control.

We've talked before about putting measures in place. Similarly, a professional gambler will set limits and know when to cut their losses and stop. It is when they chase those losses and carry on that they get into real trouble.

A professional gambler doesn't have an emotional attachment to the actual event, or even the outcome. It is a means to an overall end.

And so it is with businesses.

They are a gamble. They have risks. And sometimes they come up and sometimes they fall down.

And if they do fall down, learn from it and move on to the next one. Look at it for what it is, a vehicle to the next stage.

Don't take it personally.

> *"And I actually confronted that yesterday. There was a customer at a networking event and they were ... cool with me. I've met a couple of others since who were just much more philosophical about it and said 'Well. I took the risk. I knowingly took the risk. It was an idea and a concept and ... there you go, you know. No hard feelings.' kind of thing."*

ACTION POINT 7.2 – Don't mix business and pleasure

> *"People are different aren't they, you know? And I was a bit soft from that aspect. I was emotionally involved with the rest of the staff. You don't want to let them go because you realise that they've got families as well, you know. I should have been more ... business minded, rather than emotionally minded. I should have been a bit of a git really."*

Who do you work with?

Do you have a business partner or fellow directors?

Do you have employees that work for you? How many of them are friends or relatives?

And by friends, I don't mean someone that you just get along with. I mean real friends, that you see socially and whose families you know. People that, if it wasn't for the business, you'd be seeing anyway.

Now, remember how you and your business are two separate identities?

Well, the friends and relatives that you identified just now are only friends and relatives of you. To the business they are employees, directors, business owners, whatever.

You have to know when you are doing things for the business and when you are doing things for yourself.

There may come a time when you have to make a member of your family redundant.

Or, it may happen that your business partner has a different attitude to the business than you, due to holding different values and desires. Which could lead to differences of opinion and motivations for action which cause arguments and create fallouts. Not fun, if they are a 'friend'.

When you are making a decision, are you thinking what is best for the business or are you thinking what is best for you? The two are, often, mutually exclusive.

Are you holding off decisions that impact others because they are genuine friends, or just people that you've got to know?

You have to be clear in your own mind, if it ever comes down to it, what takes the greater priority. Preserving the business or preserving the friendship.

It may seem callous, but you have to be aware of who you are and what your role is in your business and, therefore, your responsibilities to others in given situations.

> *"Cut your staff straight away. You've got to be, you know, you got to treat ... I don't mean treat your staff like a gangrene, but treat the situation like gangrene and you've got to cut it out. You've just got to cut it. And it sounds horrible but your staff's your biggest overhead."*

Don't be afraid of insolvency

Even the healthiest companies are only one big event away from collapse. We have covered a number of reasons as to why people don't take action or plan for appropriate contingencies.

Our history and our culture is full of stories of debtors prisons and the stigma and spectre of insolvency, so no wonder we fear it and refuse to take action that may move us closer towards it.

But times have changed. It is no longer the scary beast it was and the actual event can be painless and, sometimes, even a blessing.

But there's no point me just telling you this in any detail. I'm going to step aside in this section and leave it entirely in the hands of the contributors. Their words are explanation enough.

> *"I'm out of that business. It's not taking all my time and effort, my capacity and driving me nuts. And I'm not spending my time running around after people who I'm paying lots of money to. So if I can build again without having them problems and issues, then off I go."*

"The only alternative route, it felt like, was to say 'Okay. This is what's going to happen. What we've got to do ... we've got to tell the stakeholders that despite of our best efforts this is where we're at.' That was the worst thing, I think, and then taking a couple of phone calls from them saying 'What the hell have you been doing?' and all of the horrible thoughts that you think that might happen. People are going to call you an idiot or worse. You know, feel that they've been cheated.

Without doubt, we didn't cheat anybody but I could understand how some of them would feel 'Oh, that was just a silly idea and I was an idiot for buying into it. They just took our money and ...' I mean, Christ! We hardly lived the life of luxury or anything like that. Everything was very frugal. But I can understand how people might have a different perception.

We had everything from a polite but very strongly written letter that basically said 'Thanks a lot, you wankers. What are you going to do about it? I'm really pissed off' ... which is fair enough and I think if I was to see that person they might find it hard to even speak to me ... was the feeling I got from them. Through to others who rang and or wrote and said 'Don't worry about it, it's only money. Is there anything we can do to help?'

Wow! Oh my word! Jaw dropping, you know. So in amongst anybody's group of people that they think are going to react a certain way, some will and some of them will do amazing things.

If I knew what the reaction was going to be, it would have been far easier. I think that we would have had less angst, less damage to our own selves, as people and our sense of worth and value in the world.

That a really important thing to protect no matter what you do in life. Recognition of your value in the world ... and that took a bit of a battering. A lot of a battering. So if we'd known in advance that some people would have gone 'Hey, you know what? Don't worry about it.'...

We even got a letter from one gentleman, I've still got the letter, who we didn't know, who was literally introduced to us and just made a purchase from and

£5,000 and that was that. And he wrote to us afterwards and said 'Really don't want you to be disheartened. You know. Okay, it hasn't worked. Don't stop being a pioneer. Don't stop being an innovator. In a way I congratulate you.'

And you couldn't have imagined somebody would write that kind of letter to encourage you. And if we'd known that that would have been the reaction, it would have been easier to take. To accept that it had to end."

> *"It was kind of 50% relief but then 50% of real agonising dread of 'Okay. We're going through this, but is it going to happen? How're we going to get out of this? Where are we going to be once this has happened?' And not really actually believing that this is actually possible. That you can close a company down and liquidate it and then still be left with something. And I think if I'd realised **that** sooner, how **that** would be done ... that could have come earlier.*
>
> *It was relatively easy. One set thing to say. It was just a decision ... one thing to decide. My saying 'Yes ... we'll go through this'. That could have been done a lot earlier if I'd understood that you could actually do that. Not understanding the actual legal side of things.*
>
> *And you always think 'Yeah, you know. It's gonna come back and bite me.' But the only comeback was because I'd guaranteed certain*

things. I didn't think in an insolvency you could say 'Right ... you can carry on trading ... with that name.' But how can you just do that? I didn't think it was legal. I was looking over my shoulder thinking 'I'm going to get a letter in the post tomorrow saying you've done something wrong. You'd done something illegal.' And get myself into worse trouble than what I'd done.

We just thought that we would lose everything. We would lose absolutely everything."

"*It was a relief, winding it up, really. Not winding it up, but basically putting it to bed. Because it represented failure to me.*

You end up despising it.

I just remember having a feeling of relief when we had the conversation of 'Let's stop this. Let's stop.' And even more so, quite symbolic but, packing it all up and putting

it in a box, and taping the box shut and putting it in the loft. There was something cathartic about that I think."

"*So the trauma of going through it was so horrible and if I knew now what I'd known then I would have handled it differently."*

> *"I wouldn't have been as scared to put it down. Because you think ... because it's such a humiliating experience and you think there's only you going through it and that you shouldn't be doing it. And it's the pressure ... of that.*
>
> *And wondering how it's going to end up, whether you're going to end up in jail, or whatever, because we had nobody to kind of advise us. Because we didn't know people who could advise us until I actually went and had a chat with the liquidator."*

"Don't be frightened. Have no fear, 'cos fear is the mindkiller. To go through something like that is not as bad as what you think it is at the time. If somebody could have come up to me 6 months previous and said 'You might get to a point where you've got to put it into liquidation. Don't be frightened of it. Don't be frightened of it.'

Because you actually come out of it a better person. I wouldn't say a brilliant experience, but it is a very life changing experience where you learn a lot. It improves you as a person if you handle it in the correct way. And it's this massive fear and humiliation and, you know, the knot in your stomach. Where you actually don't need to have that. You actually don't need to have that because it is happening to thousands of other businesses. And if you've run your business to the best of your ability then you have nothing to be scared of."

> *"I can remember being in the meeting when it's being delivered to you that it's happening. You realise that, you know, this is not good. You're sat there thinking 'This is not good news. I don't really like what's being said.' However, there's .. there's a certain sense of 'Well. We now know what's in the future.' And it is really bizarre to say that, but you're like, 'Well, I now know what's going to happen tomorrow. I don't have to come in and work my 12-14 hour days. I now know that tomorrow I'm going to have an easier day.' From that perspective."*

Summary

Only by fully understanding the situation can we prevent fear from affecting our actions.

Never assume how other people will react to given situations and never confuse yourself and your relationships with the business and the relationships of the business.

You have to be able to look at every option without bringing in personal motivations and emotions. If you can honestly say that what you have done is the best for the business, then you have nothing to worry about.

If, however, you do lose your business, this can have a deep psychological impact on you and your confidence going forward. The next chapter deals with this issue.

CHAPTER 8 : THE TRADITIONAL LABEL OF FAILURE

> *"Well, I think the traditional sort of perceived definition of failure is 'Oh! They've lost the house, the business has folded, they've gone bankrupt'. And, actually you can say 'So what?' to each of those statements or labels."*

In the last chapter we looked at how you are not your business and, consequently, the failure of one does not automatically equal the failure of the other.

However, the collapse of a business is such a major event, it undoubtedly has an impact on how you perceive yourself and how you imagine others will perceive you.

My business failed. I have failed. I am a failure. I will always be a failure.

How easy it is for one event in the past to impact on our attitudes to the future. This is one of the main topics of deliberation when you are floating around the LOWPOINT.

Am I a failure?

Think back in your life.

Have you ever failed an exam at school?

Taken more than one attempt to pass your driving test?

Lost a game of Monopoly to a friend or sibling?

All of these can be perceived as a failure, as will thousands of other things that have occurred in your life.

And, in each of those cases, you had a huge amount of influence over the outcome.

How much you studied. How well you drove. Your tactics and strategy on buying properties.

So, based on all of those failings in your life, does that brand you a failure?

If you think it does, then you are branding just about every person on the planet as a failure, because everyone experiences things that don't work. And the danger of just focussing on the things that didn't work, is that you paint the wrong picture.

"There's no such thing as failure."

Take Albert Einstein as an example.

During his life he failed the entrance exams to the Swiss Federal Polytechnic; was unemployed for two years after graduating; had a failed marriage; was instrumental in starting the nuclear arms race which caused the death of at least a quarter of a million people; and died having failed to crack the one last theorem that he devoted the last 6 or 7 years of his life to.

It would be very easy to look at these things and say that Einstein was a failure.

Yet we know this not to be the case and that is because we focus on the amazing things that he did achieve.

Now, obviously, we can't all come up with the theory of relativity in our spare time, but the point is that life is a series of events and we can not define who we are by a mere handful of them.

You have to look at the bigger picture and be fully aware of what successes you have enjoyed and what you truly want out of life.

> *"I think it's those typical western values. Whereas actually, failure for me, would have been not being there regularly for my daughter, not having a relationship with friends and family. That would be failure in another sense.*
>
> *We've all got some talent in us and some potential in us and not daring or trying to find it and help it grow is perhaps a form of failure."*

External perceptions

There are two elements to be taken into consideration here and it is very important that you distinguish between the two.

When your business fails, there is the stress of having to deal with how everybody else perceives you and there is the stress of having to deal with how **you think** everybody perceives you.

These two are very different.

> *"The common belief is that if the company goes down, it's because the director or the owner of the company has taken a load of money out and let the company go down. They've actually got a stack load of money in a bank account somewhere and they're going to start up again somewhere else. This is such a common misconception."*

Now, no one is going to state here that it's all in your mind and everyone actually loves you.

Sure, there will be people that lost money as a result of what happened and will be angry. There will be others that might use what happened as a reason to deal with you differently, such as a bank refusing to lend any money.

And it is genuinely possible that you will lose contact with some friends or family members.

That, however, is a reflection on them. Not on you.

THE TRADITIONAL LABEL OF FAILURE

> *"People get pissed with you. Because they've never been through it themselves, they don't understand. They don't understand how you can't do anything about it. You don't put yourself through that voluntarily. You get treated as though you have money stashed away somewhere, which I didn't have."*

In the most part you will find that family and friends will rally round and give you a huge amount of support if you let them. Anyone that thinks that you are a failure isn't someone you want to be around anyway.

> *"I think the employees were fine. They knew the truth. Some of the suppliers along with some of the competition, their reaction was ... they just thought I'd had it away with all the money. They just saw that the company's gone down, he's got a good life so he must have taken all the money."*

Just by way of example, along the lines of the Einstein example, just spend some time researching some of the famous people that 'failed' before they became 'successful'.

Go online and see how many people have either been bankrupt or had at least one business fail before they got things right. You will see that they didn't let a few setbacks impact on their future.

And that is the key thing. Yes, it might be unpleasant for a time, but it is only for a time.

> *"My dad was extremely supportive and reminded me that the bank withdrew funds from him in 1974 and he had a very hard ride. And yet floated a business in 1984. So he was saying is 'Don't worry. Basically, there are many many wealthy businessmen who have got a bust company behind them. And you must remember it was a limited company for good reason.'*
>
> *And I think that is an extremely valid point and that is something that a lot of businessmen, including me, forgot."*

What defines you as a person is not what happens to you, but how you behave.

A Guilty Complex

> *"When you've been through that, it's difficult to get back on again, isn't it? You feel like you've shafted your suppliers, you've shafted the bank and all your employees. Everything you've worked towards ... you've completely wiped the floor with all of that. So to stand up and get back on and start another company doing exactly the same thing, bearing in mind your customers have gone down the Swanee as well. It's very difficult."*

THE TRADITIONAL LABEL OF FAILURE

We all get into business for our own reasons and are driven by personal motivations but, whatever those 'selfish' elements are, the only way to get on in business is to form good relationships with the people you work with.

We tend to work well with the people we get on with and so we establish strong bonds with employees, suppliers and customers to the point where some of them become friends on a personal level.

When your business collapses there will be creditors that lose money, customers whose orders are unfulfilled, employees that lose jobs and questions raised about your intentions and personal morals.

We can imagine what it is like to be one of those people because we have often been there ourselves. Many of us are familiar with the sensations that arise when a customer goes bust owing a lot of money and how it can impact on other things. Now, you are doing that to someone else.

Many people do their utmost to ensure that the smaller companies and the employees are impacted as little as possible. Often to their own detriment.

However, it doesn't remove the feelings of guilt that can arise from letting all these friends and associated down.

Get a sense of perspective

Before we proceed, I want to make something clear. The next few exercises are aimed at reducing the levels of guilt you feel.

This is not with the intention of turning you into a callous, single minded robot that only does things that benefits themselves. The intention is to merely redress the balance a bit, as we tend to let these things swing too far in favour of others and it can have a crippling effect on our future behaviours.

> *"It's probably taken the last two years to feel like I can come out in the business world, the business public. And if I meet somebody who has a view of then and what happened ... it's okay. I can sit down with them if they've a mind to and say 'Look, that's how it is.' So I feel like I'm out of my cave and back into public.*
>
> *Some people might want to throw some mud, some people might not ... whatever it is, I don't mind. It's okay. I've managed to redress my perspective."*

So, by all means feel a twinge of guilt and aim to do right by others in the future. If you want to use it as motivation to get up and running again, then that is fantastic. But if you are letting it overwhelm you and it is making you hard to step outside your front door, then the balance has to swing back a little.

ACTION POINT 8.1 – Be comfortable with your business failure

The first thing you need to do to step away from your guilt, is to spend some time analysing why you set up the business in the first place.

> *"A lot of self examination of whether my motives were right in what we were trying to achieve with the business. Because that's what was at the core of what we said to people about what we were trying to achieve and they bought into that idea, which was a sound business model that ticked a lot of boxes in terms of environmentalism and social responsibility and innovation ... being profitable. All those, you know. So I think just a lot of self examination and whether our motives were right, which they were, and whether we misled anybody about what we were doing and how we were doing it ... we didn't.*
>
> *So, in spite of ... in the traditional sense of what was a really bad result, ultimately some good has come from it from a learning experience.*
>
> *I recognise that 'You know what, you just tried something that nobody had ever tried before and, okay ... it worked ... to a point and then was unable to carry on working ... and would it have been super successful? and we're not going to know.' But that's what you were trying*

> *to do. You were trying to do something that nobody had ever done before and there's some value in that."*

If, on reflection, you were in business for the wrong reasons and behaved in a selfish and borderline illegal manner, then you have found some learning points for how not to behave in the future.

However, the fact that you're reading this book suggests that you are not that person. More than likely you had the best of intentions and thought that you were doing right by people.

Sure, you may have made some mistakes. Welcome to the club on that one. But be honest. Stick your hand in the air and admit to it and make sure you don't make that particular mistake again.

> *"There's nothing wrong with being wrong, is there? There's nothing wrong with being wrong. Just put your hands up. Get the help or make the decision and move on from it."*

But don't undermine what your intentions were. If your intentions were fundamentally sound, then you can hold your head up high and be proud of what you attempted to achieve.

Now go on and make the next thing work.

ACTION POINT 8.2 – How have you helped others?

You feel devastated.

All the employees with families to feed and that depended on you for money have lost their jobs and an income.

Customers that were looking to you for supply have been let down and had to rearrange everything, possibly at a cost.

Suppliers are owed money they will never get back, which could seriously impact on their own businesses.

How do you cope with the guilt here?

Well, obviously you could take a fairly pragmatic point of view. The other companies are in business themselves, so they too are gamblers and are responsible for their own welfare. It's not your job to sort out their controls and to ensure that they stay afloat.

Besides, it's not like you've come out of this unscathed.

> *"Overall, I was the biggest creditor, 'cos I had about £60,000 personal debt for loans and things like that. In fact, if you totted them all up, the people who were left in liquidation, I*

had more debt than all of them put together. Plus I had all the stress of dealing with it."

But I can see you might think that that's a bit cold. Here's something else that might help.

Let's start with the suppliers.

How long have you been trading with them? And over that time, how much business have you placed with them?

Try and estimate how much money you've paid to them over all your years of business.

You may not know what their profit margins are, but have a stab at guessing how much of that business converted into bottom line profits.

So, how much money have they made out of you over the years?

Check again how much money you owe them now. Oh, and you can deduct from that figure the estimated profit margin, as that is how much they are really out of pocket for.

Overall, are they better off or worse off after being in business with you?

Even if they are worse off, has the amount been mitigated by this analysis?

This is not something that you want to use as an

argument with them, but it can help you gain a perspective on the real situation and not leave you quite so beholden to them in the future.

You can do a similar exercise with your employees. Not quite so easy as with suppliers as the personal element is a lot stronger.

However, it may provide some slight relief if you consider how much money they have earned from you over the years.

> *"You get some business owners who are totally arbitrary and don't give a damn about anybody and are totally callous. I don't mind those people suffering a little bit. [Laughs] But the genuine guys who try to run a business and, you know, when you're employing ten people. That's ten families, you know, you're helping to keep.*
>
> *So, when you've done that ... you've actually done something really, really good. And the fact that it hasn't worked, but you've worked it to the best of your ability rather than being tough with negligence, then you shouldn't really fear. You've got nothing to fear"*

Honesty

There is only really one way to power through any remaining guilt factors. And that is by being honest.

Be open with your suppliers, your customers and your employees about what you've done and why you've done it. Admit to mistakes and apologise when necessary, but always tell the truth.

> *"I rang a few of them up. Our biggest creditor, I personally knew the financial director there. Rang him up, told him what was happening. And we managed to pay them as much as we possibly could and when we set up the new company, they gave us an account straight away because of the past relationship, we'd been so straight and honest with them."*

Some won't be able to accept it. Some will stay angry with you and never speak to you again. But, on the whole, you will hold their trust and respect and, more than likely, their support in the future.

> *"I also felt very, very protective towards my existing customers. And all of a sudden I'd let them down. I've still got some of those customers even now. Even to this day, many years later I still deal with those people. 'Cos ... just honesty more than anything. Just honesty. As honest as you can be with anybody. You know."*

ACTION POINT 8.3 – Reassess success

> *"Similarly you might ponder 'What is success?'. There's the conventional definition of financial*

> *success and maybe social standing or stuff like that, I guess, but for me you become successful the very moment that you start moving towards a worthwhile goal. So if somebody says 'Are you successful?' my answer would be 'Yes'. Because I feel that I am working towards a worthwhile goal.*
>
> *And that would apply to anybody really. And that's not necessarily financial or commercial or anything like that. It's just about your values, isn't it, and your philosophy and what you give, I guess."*

Many common things cropped up in the conversations that I held with people, but this is one thing that was the same for absolutely everyone. And that was their reassessment of what they felt to be important in life.

It didn't matter if they'd been millionaires and lost it or never made it out of their two bed flat. Money, cars, houses and material things are no longer what drives any of them.

> *"I will know that I'm successful ... well, there's two things really. There's a certain lifestyle, which isn't as opulent as I thought it would be two or three years ago. It's more based on what I'm doing on a week to week basis. And I have to say, I'm kind of almost there. It's two things, it's a certain way of living and it's ... er ... an*

assurance and knowing in my own mind that ... my self esteem is where I want it to be."

It's time for you to really think about what success means to you.

1. Go back to your list from earlier about the things that are important to you

2. Check to see if there is anything you need to add or subtract.

3. Spend time listing out all of the positive things that you **have** done in each area

4. What points can you learn from mistakes that you have made

5. For each area, be really clear with yourself what you want to achieve and why. What are the end goals for each item?

6. Write down how you will know, overall, when you have been 'successful'.

Look at what you've written down and think about how it makes you feel. If you feel positive and excited, then good. You have the right focus.

If it seems scary, then that's good too, as long as the fear isn't crippling. If the thought is too much for you, then rein it in a bit. We need to get small steps going in the first instance and don't want you stopping before you start.

THE TRADITIONAL LABEL OF FAILURE

> *"The trouble is, when you're down there [points to floor]... you still set your goals up there [points to ceiling]. You've really got to chunk everything down. Instead of like going straight for that [ceiling] ... chunk it down. So, what are you gonna do to get there [about halfway in between].*
>
> *It's development, nice and steady. Don't set expectations for yourself. Don't set your goals too high. We've all got to have goals, but don't set them too high. Just work through them steady."*

And if you aren't inspired by what you've written go back and see what you might have missed out of the process. If you've identified things that are important to you and what you perceive as success in each of those areas, then you should be motivated by it.

> *"Money's not everything. I naturally don't believe that it is anymore. Success is the respect that you earn from your peers and your family and the love that you get from members of your family. And just being happy. Happiness is not about ... it's not a journey. Happiness is a state of mind or it's a way of life. So I believe ... God I sound so ... I'm an Evangelist! [laughs]. I just ... you just think differently . I just think differently now."*

By understanding what success now means to you, you will find it easier to avoid the label of failure.

Comparison caveat

It is very common for friends and family to say things like 'Just think, there's always somebody worse off than you'.

Comparing yourself against other people that are facing difficulties can be a way of getting perspective.

> *"I mean crikey, yeah, [talking about a mutual associate]. I've never met her, but she's had cancer and she's got zero money coming in 'cos she's not in a position where she can go out and do something about it.*
>
> *Oof, that's hard. You know, going bankrupt, losing some houses and needing to start over again is hard ... but it's not as hard as that. Not compared to that, you know."*

However, I found that this approach could actually have a negative impact if the mindset of the individual was not in the right place. It ends up throwing an extra dose of guilt into the mix.

> *"It might be a massive thing in your head. If you see stuff on telly, I tell you, that's not good.*
>
> *You see starving kids on the telly you're thinking*

> *'Why the hell have I got depression? Why am I feeling shit because my business went, when these can't eat?'*
>
> *So then it starts heaping more stuff on to you. And it makes you feel **worse**. Because you're feeling sorry for yourself and there's kids that can't eat. You know what I mean? If your mindset is like that."*

Summary

This is important.

The longer you take wallowing in self pity; blaming yourself for the downfall of your company and how it affected others; thinking yourself a failure and worried about what others will think of you, the longer it will take for you to emerge and move on.

Get some context of the situation and then think about what success really means to you.

Once you understand that, you can work out what you need to get going again.

The next common issue, which we will look at next, is the level of self confidence. Your ability to run a company has just been tested and found wanting.

How do you pick yourself back up, move out of the LOWPOINT and rebuild those confidence levels?

CHAPTER 9 : GETTING BACK ON THE HORSE

> *"A lot of self doubt. A lot of 'Can I really do it?' A lot of lack of confidence. A lot of all that stuff. And the problem is coming back. Everyone you meet, everybody treats you like shit. They think, because I went into liquidation, I'm some sort of idiot. They're gonna find out different."*

Once you start getting back into working circles, that will instil a bunch of self confidence in itself. We will look at those working options in the next chapter. Before then, however, you need to take the first few steps to RE-EMERGENCE. These are vital in order to get the virtuous circle moving.

Remember, all of this is a lot easier if you have someone there to help you through the process.

> *"It takes a long time. You've got to ... I would say with a considerable amount of support. I had to have intense counselling basically to keep my mind in the right place. Because you do start to think 'Well, I'm a bit knackered. I'm living in a flat with negative equity; I still have to visit my ex-wife with a bloody multi-million pound house with no mortgage with millions in the bank. I've now got no business. Everybody who speaks to me asks me what happened with the company 'We thought you were really good and really strong.' You know, you're signing on*

the dole.' There's not a lot of positivity in your life.

Thankfully my friends and family were saying 'Take your time. Lick your wounds and come back'."

ACTION POINT 9.1 – Take proper time to mourn the loss of your business

Losing your business is like losing a child. Something you have nurtured and grown from an infant suddenly gets snatched away from you, never to be seen again.

"I don't know. It's almost when a relative dies. At least you feel a slight relief that at least you know where you are."

Take the time to properly grieve for that business. Get upset. Cry. Rant. Rave. Whatever you need to do to vent the emotions.

But don't let it consume you.

One piece of advice that was suggested was to treat the grieving process as you would a job. Put aside some hours a day, 9 to 5 even or whatever suits, to do your thinking and your grieving. And limit your grieving time to that period.

Afterwards, go out in the evening, down the pub with some friends or the cinema. Or stay at home and watch television Whatever, but switch off from the negative for some of the time.

If you can get into a routine (and make notes of all your thoughts and ideas) you will find it easier to sleep and stay on top of things.

At the same time, go through the exercise in the previous chapter and get comfortable with the reasons why the business failed.

> *"One of the other problems that I have, and I think a lot of owners have, is that the reason why you're probably an owner is that you never switch off. Your brain is calculating all the time and your brain, it's a bit like a computer, it was overheating. I was trying to calculate 'How have you done this? How have you managed to go from being essentially rich and having no money worries at all to signing on in the dole office? How have you done that?' And your brain calculates it all the time."*

Which things were caused by elements completely outside of your control?

Which things were genuine mistakes that you made that caused the downfall?

Recognise that mistakes happen. What's important is that you learn from those mistakes.

Be comfortable with your intentions for the

business itself and your intentions when in charge of the business.

Find a phrase the nicely summarises what happened in case anyone asks you. Not a guilt trip. Not a blame game.

> *"That knocks your confidence to a huge extent, particularly with your suppliers because you've spent a long time generating those relationships. Some of those people I'd known for 10 years. So it's very difficult to have the confidence to get back on and it sounds very hollow when you're blaming other factors rather than yourself."*

Something accurate and concise – followed by your learning point.

For example:

Concerned individual - "I hear you lost your business. What happened?"

You - "I didn't spot a massive shift in the market place. I can tell you, going forward I'll be watching things like a hawk."

Or - "The recession damaged us, but it was the fact that I didn't downsize as much as I should have done that killed us. From now on, I'll be running with a much more flexible workforce."

Or - "We were taken out by a massive bad debt. That's the last time I put all my eggs in one basket."

> *"It takes you a good year to, I would say at least a year, to mentally get to the point of saying 'Well that was just a limited company. Circumstances got me. Sure there were things I did wrong, but that don't mean to say you can't do something in the future.'*
>
> *You've got to get your brain into that arena to be able to be receptive to that idea and stop mourning the end of the bloody business."*

ACTION POINT 9.2 – Change your language

How you're feeling inside is reflected in the way you speak. Conversely, the way you speak can influence the way you feel inside.

The more you talk about 'failing', 'fear', 'impossible', 'try' or anything with a negative connotation, the more you are going to feel negative and the harder it will be to do anything.

> *"And I also firmly believe that the more you verbalise your thoughts, somehow the more tangible and real they become.*
>
> *So, if you find yourself saying 'We'll have to see how things go with the business' about a holiday ... if you say it enough, it almost becomes your belief set and it almost becomes*

THE TRADITIONAL LABEL OF FAILURE

a bit self fulfilling then.

And what you verbalise, affects how you think. And how you think affects how you behave. And the actions you take determine your outcome.

Language is so powerful and the correct usage of language. You have to be thoughtful about that sometimes. When you say to a kid:

'Don't fall out of that tree!'

the picture in their brain is 'Falling out of the tree'. Being able to remember in advance and say to the child:

'Climb that tree safely.'

which puts a different picture in your mind and the child's mind. It's a skill you have to ... because naturally we don't speak like that. And so that's what I'm sort of saying.

So your language and the pictures that creates is very important and it is very easy when things start to get on top of you a bit that your language and the thoughts you create for yourself and your expectations begin to be on a downward negative tract and thus because they're more that way, you become more that way."

The more you talk about 'success', 'opportunities', 'possibilities', 'do' or anything with positive elements, so you will feel more positive.

Get someone close to you to look out for your language and pick you up on any negative self talk. Get into the habit of talking positively and your mood will change as well.

ACTION POINT 9.3 – Celebrate your successes

With your positive language in place, take another look at your business.

You've acknowledged where mistakes have happened but you've learnt from them.

You've gained comfort that you were in business for the right reasons.

Now take a look at all the things that you did that went well. That worked. That were positive and successful. There will be a lot of things.

> *"Look at things in a completely different light. To give you an example of that, I remember going to one session with this remarkable lady. She's incredible. And I was saying that I feel really gutted that I'm now staring bankruptcy in the face and there's my ex-wife a multi-millionaire. And she's never worked. And I found it really, really hard to understand.*

And she basically said, 'Well. If your wife is really tight' (and she was) 'and your intention was to make sure that your wife and kids were financially secure. You've achieved that goal. You may have seen yourself in those plans, but you've still achieved that goal. Chances are that your wife will leave the money to the children, so you've also achieved that goal.

So really, it's almost a selfish attitude that you're displaying. That you're only saying it's a shame because **you're** *not experiencing it. But you've actually achieved your goals.'*

And I know it's hard to take at the time, you're thinking 'Bloody hell, that's a bit of a strange one isn't it?', but you realise that 'You're probably right' and that you **have** *achieved a lot of the goals a lot of people couldn't achieve, but it's almost you ... it's getting your brain to understand that you always thought you were in it. But is it really that important whether you're in it or not? As long as the woman that you love for many years and your children are secure. Which is what you achieved.*

So you do start to look at life differently.

Someone said 'If I had to pick a scenario where you say you're going to go through this horrendous time. Are you prepared to live in a flat and have no income, but in return we

> *safeguard your wife and kids?' You would take it every time."*

If you focus on all of the negative things, then the enterprise will feel negative to you.

> *"The difficulty is coming back up. Because you kind of feel in a way that maybe you've ... well you get a big shock. 'Cos you get a big shock that you're not as good as what you think you are. Coming back up after that, a lot of people never do it."*

Yet this is only a tiny part of the whole.

Remember all the good times, the big wins, the tough negotiations that you won and you start to build a better perspective.

Feel more positive about what you've done.
Feel more positive about the business.
Feel more positive about yourself.

ACTION POINT 9.4 – Get out

You've done your stint mourning. You're feeling better about yourself and talking a good game.

Now just get out of the house.

> *"If you don't do something. What was the point of all of that if you don't do something and take from it the lessons you can take from it?"*

THE TRADITIONAL LABEL OF FAILURE

Meet with friends; join a sports club; go networking.

> *"Started going to the gymnasium again. You know. Started to work on 'me'. Give yourself more time. I wanted 'me' back.*
>
> *I've always liked myself, because I like my own company. But I didn't like the person that were ... I were looking in the mirror at, and I were talking to. 'Cos he were just dead. There were no spirit inside him.*
>
> *So I started going to the gym, cut down on alcohol, stopped smoking. I started working at giving 'me' a bit back. Rather than business, bloody business, business, business, business, business.*
>
> *And that turned it."*

Whatever small steps you need to get talking to people, moving in social circles and generally becoming a member of society again.

> *"Get out of that shell. Because people feel comfortable as soon as they get into that little zone. It's their comfort zone. And get 'em out of that comfort zone and do something else."*

Once you become a member of society again, you can start worrying about what you do for work again.

Summary

Despite all of the precautions and support you may get, losing a business to insolvency hurts.

Rushing back too quickly can cause even more damage if your mindset is not in the right place. So take your time and get all that grieving and self reflection out of your system.

But always keep an eye on the learning point and the positive angle.

Be mindful of the good things you have done, understand your strengths and what you can do about your weaknesses and keep mixing with people.

It might be hard, but it will be worthwhile.

Now to move your thoughts away from your **ability** to do things and onto what you actually do next.

CHAPTER 10 : WHAT AM I GOING TO DO NEXT?

We've talked about the fear of an insolvency and the fear of failure. Another massive area is the fear around what to do once the company goes into insolvency.

> *"So, one minute I'm owning a business and the next minute 'What am I going to do next?'*
>
> *When I meet clients now and I'm talking to them about stuff and I meet that 'thing'. Because I've been there I know what's going through their mind. And what's going through their mind is 'What am I going to do next?'. You know.*
>
> *'I've got to change. I don't like it. Grumble grumble'.*
>
> *And I went through all that stuff."*

When you have been so involved with one business and one industry for so long, losing all of that can be incredibly daunting. How do you take a step forward when you don't know what you're stepping towards?

> *"But, you know, where do you go from there? What is the 'next'. Okay, we stopped and we closed our business down. We stopped doing it, but where do we ... and this is all I know. And*

that's the hardest thing. People will enjoy the business they're doing. But where do I go now? Where am I going to earn my living?"

In this chapter, I want to look at some of the options that you can explore that will help you RE-EMERGE and take you towards that picture of success that you painted for yourself earlier.

ACTION POINT 10.1 - Same or similar

Most people stick with what they know. If they've been in plastics all their life, then plastics is where they will stay.

Absolutely nothing wrong with that, as long as they want to be in plastics rather than staying there **purely** because that's what they know. More of that later.

So, assuming you want to stay doing a similar sort of thing, what can you do?

Well, here are a few options, the viability of which will depend on the type of business and your personal position:

- Support the insolvency practitioner until it is sold;

- If the business is sold to a third party, they may need your help to run it;

- You can buy the business back from the

insolvency practitioner and carry on trading;

- You can buy a portion of the assets and take forward just the profitable division;
- Just start up a new company doing the same thing as before.

To fully understand how these options can work, it helps to have a basic understanding of corporate structures and insolvency practices. In order not to bore those people that are fully up to speed with these business practicalities, if you need some background on these matters then email me on andrew@businessenjoyment.com and I'll send you a pdf titled "What Happens in an Insolvency?"

Support the insolvency practitioner

If the company goes into administration and is traded for a period of time whilst a buyer is found, a good option is to stay close and help out as much as possible.

As a director of the company, you are obliged to assist anyway, however, there are degrees to which that assistance can be given. The suggestion here is that you be as proactive as possible, actively working with the insolvency practitioner to achieve the optimum result for the business.

Forging a good relationship with the insolvency practitioner may not impact on what you do next, but it will make things easier for you if you want to stay involved in your business going forward.

Yes, it is only a short term arrangement and you may not be able to rely on any bridges you build, but at least those bridges will be there. By not burning them, it keeps a number of options open to you.

Even if your role is purely to help collect debtors in for them (which will be of particular interest if you have a personal guarantee to the bank, as this will help reduce the amount you owe), be as helpful as you can.

The benefit to you is that you will be closer to what is going on with the business, have an idea as to any parties that may be looking to buy it and create goodwill with some people that have good contacts within the business world.

However, your mind may well be elsewhere during this phase, so do pay attention to your personal state.

Third party sale

If a competitor takes on your business and integrates it into their own, there is very little likelihood that they will need your services going forward.

There may be some specific issues that they will need help on, so there may be an opportunity for a short term consulting role. That will at least bring some money in whilst you work on your next options.

However, it is not uncommon for a purchaser to take on the business and need someone to run it, even if they are a competitor.

You may well be naturally placed to fill that role anyway, but they are more likely to think about you and ask for your help if you are in the forefront of their minds.

That is why Option 1 is so important, as your continued presence in the business will increase your chances of staying involved.

This will, of course, probably mean that you will be employed by somebody else in your own business, instead of running it yourself. So you have to think hard as to what is more important at this stage. Income or status?

Buy the business back

The insolvency practitioner is looking to get as much money as they can for the assets of the company. That includes selling the business as a whole.

Remember, this is a sale of the assets, not of the company. Consequently, the buyer will take on any premises, machinery etc, plus the order book and customer list. Everything that is needed to continue trading the business, but they do not take on the liability of the creditors (other than employees).

The insolvency practitioner's ideal would be to have two or three competing bids from third parties as this is likely to lead to a higher offer.

However, there are a number of reasons as to why a director can lead a bid that will be the best on the table.

Firstly, if there are no other interested parties, any sensible offer that the director makes will be preferable to a break-up of the business.

Secondly, there may be unknowns or uncertainties lying in the company that put other parties off, lowering their bids. For example, a property developing company will have a number of projects that require absolute confidence on planning permissions, costs to complete and knowledge of hidden problems that may come to the fore in the future.

A third party purchaser will have a very limited time to do any due diligence and any areas of uncertainty will be treated as a reason for reducing the price.

As the director of the company, you should know the business inside out and have much greater faith in what is contained therein, which would allow you to put in a higher bid than parties with less information.

There is, naturally, a question of funding. Many banks don't fund phoenix companies as a matter of course.

However, there are innumerable companies out there that are set up specifically to help fund these sort of deals.

Speak to the insolvency practitioner and tell them that you are interested in putting an offer in for the business, but need some help in putting a bid together and raising finance.

They will put you in touch with the right people for your type of business.

It will probably mean that you then step away from the business to avoid any conflicts or perceived conflicts regarding your bid. Other interested parties may take a dim view to you being involved with the business when you have an ulterior motive, regardless of your actual intentions.

This is a very common way forward, but you have to be very careful about what you are prepared to risk to buy your business back. Pay special attention to how much control you are giving away to your new funders and any personal guarantees that are required.

Buy part of the business back

If taking back the whole business is too expensive, too risky or something that you just aren't interested in doing then, assuming no-one else is interested in taking it on, there may be a halfway house that could work for you.

You do have the option of just buying the assets at break-up value. However, you are not able to use this merely as a way of escaping employee liabilities. Laws are in place to ensure that, whatever the wording in a contract, if you essentially take on the business, you take on the employees as well (with service records intact).

However, if your business can be broken down into definable divisions or sections, it is possible to take on just one of those divisions as a separate entity. You still take on the employees, but only those relevant to that division.

Here are some examples that illustrate the situation:

- For any retail operations, the online section may be separate;

- If there is a manufacturing division and a servicing/spare parts division, one of them may stand alone as a viable business;

- With geographically separate offices one or more may be run as its own entity. This includes multi-store retailers;

- There may be a long term contracts division for which sales, employees and processes are clearly identifiable; or
- If the business is just organised in different teams, there may be a way of splitting them out.

The point is to be creative. Again, the insolvency practitioner will be happy to work with you on this if there isn't any sign of a full sale, as it will be a better alternative to a complete break up.

As a general rule, the more jobs you can save via a purchase, the better the offer is likely to be and, therefore, the more interested the insolvency practitioner will be.

This isn't always the case and the cash offer still has to be higher than any break up valuation, but it isn't a bad rule of thumb to work by.

Where the alternative is the loss of all jobs and the closure of the business, this can be the best compromise available.

Start again

If you can't raise enough funding to buy all or part of the business back, what then?

Well, have a careful think about what the business

actually is and what you'd be getting from an asset sale anyway.

There is a tendency to get blinded by the emotions of your own company and what it means to you. But if you take away the attraction of the familiar, what do you actually need?

If it is physical assets, then which of these are available elsewhere? How many do you actually need to get a basic operation running again?

If it is knowledge and knowhow, how much of that is in your head? Where are there gaps and who do you know that can plug them? Are they available for a discussion about a new venture?

Where it is customer and supplier relationships, how many of them have you maintained? Who would still be happy to deal with you if you were to start up again?

> *"Your good customers will stay with you. And those people who you share your experiences with. You'll build up lifelong relationships with those people, because they will, in some cases, sympathise and empathise with you. If you're honest with your suppliers and you try, personally.*
>
> *I still deal with suppliers who I personally owed money to because I've gone to them and said 'Look, over the next few years I will continue to*

> *deal with you. Increase your prices and I will try and give you some money back that way. And I have still remained firm friends with those people because of that. And they still deal with me now."*

If the only problem is funding, who do you know that would want to become a partner with you? Start with the list of answers from the previous questions.

There may not be a solution going down this route or, even if there is, you may not be prepared to commit to what is required, but don't assume it's a dead end without fully exploring it.

> *"I had a couple of meetings with the liquidator. And he said 'Look, there's fifty odd thousand companies go bust every year. You're just a tiny little tadpole compared with the rest of them. Don't worry about it. Just pick up. Start up again and get on with it. The government would much prefer you to do that than be a parasite on the government.' So we did"*

What's in a name?

A couple of things on the name of your company going forward.

Legal issues

Some people are concerned about starting again

and using the same company name, or very similar, to the previous one.

Indeed, there is a law in place designed to prohibit directors from starting up again as a new venture and masquerading as the now defunct company.

This law only actually applies in very specific circumstances and rarely tested, but the golden rule is, be honest. As long as you are not trying to pass yourself off as the previous company and gain benefits from existing contracts and relationships without disclosing what has happened, then you will be okay.

If you are concerned at all, ensure that the new company name is clearly different.

Another simple way is to send a blanket letter or email to your suppliers and customers, something that may be worth doing anyway as a new company, and make it clear in that letter what has happened.

The law is there to stop fraudulent activity and if you are being honest, then you have little to worry about.

Branding issues

On the other hand, some people get too attached to the company name.

Where the name is based around your own (e.g.

Andrew R Miller Ltd) then you can pretty much do what you like, as it's you.

But where you have spent years building up a brand around a name, it is very easy to get precious around it.

Try and be very objective about how important that brand name is.

Generally, unless you have a huge company with a national profile, most people couldn't care a less. Brand loyalty only really applies in supermarkets, fashion, cars etc.

If you are a local engineering firm or a regional construction company, no-one cares what your name is. The issue will be a combination of quality and price, and that's all there is to it.

By getting caught up in preserving a previous name, directors can waste a huge amount of time and money for no purpose.

If you get it, great. If not, also great. Nothing wrong with a re-brand.

> *"I spent ages trying to get back the name. I'd spent so long building it up and was proud of what it stood for in the market place. When I found out that I couldn't have it, I was annoyed.*

In the end, I picked a new name. There was nothing fancy about it. Just picked up a word I liked. And what I found out was interesting.

No-one cared what I was called. All that mattered was the price and the quality of the product. I wish I hadn't wasted so much time worrying."

Phoenix concerns

There can be a lot of reputation issues around directors setting up a new business out of the ashes of the old one.

These are usually around the intentions of the director towards the company's creditors and employees, and the level to which it was deliberate.

There is only one way to deal with this situation and we've touched on it before.

But the pride to one side, go and meet the most important people face to face and be honest.

Tell them the whole story. How you got into trouble and what your plans are going forward. If you've inconvenienced them, then apologise.

If you want to ensure that they recover their losses than make an offer.

Be careful not to over offer and wreck your new business for the sake of the old, but if you feel that the right thing to do is to honour a previous contract or be overcharged by a supplier until they recoup their losses and your business can stand it, then make whatever deal you are happy with.

The same goes with employees.

Even if you have taken on only part of the business, which means the loss of some employees, go and talk to them. Apologise and explain and promise to do what you can to help.

They may not listen. They may be angry and dismissive.

But if your intentions are genuine, then all you can do is be honest. After that it is up to other people.

> *"I'm picking all the best things out of the old company and acknowledging what was not so good. So we are far more streamlined, we are far more dynamic on the computers and the systems and the procedures. Even though we're still very small I am using all the big company ideas. We're using all the company systems that we had there.*
>
> *So I'm picking up all the good things and trying to ditch the office politics and all the negative stuff. I am disciplining myself to make sure that I remain focussed in the business."*

ACTION POINT 10.2 - Doing something different

For some of you, recent events might be a blessing in disguise. What are your genuine thoughts as regards to going back into the same industry?

Not the same company, but doing the same thing somewhere else with different people?

> *"I really tried to keep it in the trade and I suddenly ... I suppose I suddenly had a dawn of realisation that I suddenly had this freedom. I could do anything."*

If the thought turns your stomach, then maybe it's time to get out there and try something new.

> *"A lot of people, I do think, get stuck into jobs that, if they hadn't just fallen into a place of that job, they'd be doing something else. But they haven't as yet found it.*
>
> *The world must function better if everybody's in the place that they really do enjoy and they do really enjoy the work. And I didn't realise in life how many people actually don't enjoy their work."*

Dispel some myths

We're in a recession. There are no jobs. No-one hires people over 40. 60% of new businesses fail after the first year. Stick with what you know. No-one's interested in a failure.   And so on and so on and so on.

Any of that sound familiar?

Classic phrases used by you, by family, by friends, by the media and anyone that thinks they know best and likes to focus on the negative.

And it's all rubbish.

Well, mostly. It is certainly true for those people that listen to it and believe it. They then go on to make it happen, thereby making it true.

And these are the ones that the media and the stats focus on.

> *"And don't talk about recession. Seriously, do not talk about it. Don't listen to the news. I never listen to the news. Don't read the papers. Don't get yourself into that situation. 'Cos if you go to work thinking there's a recession on, nothing's gonna come through, is it? Just grasp what little positives there are."*

Let's take a recession, for example.

The country may be in recession, but this is only an average reflection of the situation.

> *"Beware of averages. A man with his head in the oven and his feet in the freezer is, on average, the right temperature."*

Consequently there are always plenty of businesses thriving at any one time, they just don't get as much press.

That doesn't mean it will be easy. A lot of hard work may be involved to get there, but it is certainly possible.

So shut off the negative thoughts. Don't listen to the nay-sayers. Stop reading the papers.

Start with a blank piece of paper (metaphorically and literally) and decide what you want to do, then see how you go about doing it.

What do you want?

In previous exercises, you should have spent some time thinking about what is important to you and what sort of lifestyle you want to have. Hopefully the big houses and the flash cars have been replaced by more down to earth needs, involving family and friends.

If you need to spend more time on the exercise, then do so. Really get clear in your head a **realistic** picture of the lifestyle you would like to lead at some point in the future.

Try and roughly calculate how much you need to be earning to fund that ideal lifestyle. Don't worry about adjusting for inflation or anything like that, just what you need to earn to cover mortgage, living costs, holidays, pension payments etc.

Your aim is to get an idea as to how much you need to be earning on an annual basis, either through employment or as a business owner, to satisfy that lifestyle.

When you've worked it out, is it a scary figure? Or is it inspiring? Or both?

If just the former, go back and check you really want everything that you've included in your image. If you want it hard enough, you'll work for it. Otherwise, do you really need it?

Scary is fine, as long as it is motivating as well. So keep working on your image until you get to a figure that you want to work towards.

We're no closer to knowing what to do next, but we do know what it needs to be able to earn to give you what you want, which is pretty important.

So, let us imagine that there is something out there: a job; a business; a vocation; whatever, that will earn you that amount of money on a regular basis.

Let us also, quite sensibly, assume that you are not going to find it right away.

The question is, how long do you have to find it?

There are two routes

You have the option of spending all your time in the immediate future, focussed purely on finding your ideal vocation.

Alternatively, you can do whatever it takes just to earn some money in order to live and then spend the rest of your time working out what you want.

So, what are your current priorities? Earning money or finding an ideal vocation?

Have a think about other incomes you may have coming into your household and savings you may have stashed away and estimate how long you can carry on at your current spending without you earning a single penny.

Make sure you really know what you are currently spending your money on and look for any savings that you can make in the short term. Then see what the gap is between income and outgoings and at what point the tank runs dry.

For some, that may be a few months, longer even. For others, it may be just a few days.

If you can spend two or three months devoted purely to finding your ideal career, it is worth doing? Otherwise, you probably want to focus on just earning some money.

Just earn some money

We are not talking about a career here.

This is doing whatever it takes just to earn some money, but leave you enough time to work on setting up your new business, seeking out a new life or whatever.

> *"A lot of it is down to your attitude and what you think you can do and what's possible to do. You know. If you watch the Apprentice. It's quite ... I actually find that quite an inspiring programme. I mean there's a lot of, you know, hyperbole in it. But it's, erm, like I mean, I think this week's where they're just going out getting rubbish and selling it.*
>
> *My wife said on a few occasions when things got pretty tough 'What are we going to do?' and I'm saying 'Look, there's always something.' "*

This probably means that you are going to work for somebody else, rather than have your own enterprise. But it is only temporary, so how long are you able to do something you don't want to do, in order to get what you want?

Now, if you are doing something just to earn money, then what you do is virtually irrelevant. It is how much you make that is important.

From the previous exercise, you should know how

much money you need to cover your basic bills. That tells you what your take home pay needs to be.

Add on 25% to roughly take tax into account and that will give you your gross figure (assuming you are a UK tax payer in the lower bands).

You now know what hourly/weekly/monthly rate you need to be earning to meet basic needs. Anything above that is a bonus.

Now it's just a combination of looking through papers, online job hunts and thinking a bit creatively in order to earn the level of money in that you need.

> *"I could do anything. But I didn't have the finances in place anymore that I did do previously. So ... I mean, what I did personally was I went up to the Lakes and I literally worked cash in hand. So I just disappeared and had this cathartic sort of period."*

I can't be too prescriptive because everyone is in a different location and a different situation, but here are some tips.

Swallow your pride (again) – you're doing this to get some essential cash in. No-one really cares what you were doing before. Don't be so proud as to think that it is beneath you to stack shelves, work in a cafe or go round knocking on doors. This is only temporary.

Alternatively, whilst you aren't working, unemployment benefits are available to you.

> *"You're in a state of shock. Because the problem with owning a business is that you lose your salary, you lose your shareholder's funds. You really are cast adrift and you've no idea what to do. I had a huge maintenance payment on me, something like 60 or 70 grand a year. I was still having to honour that, so the legal advice was 'We'd like you to go on the dole. Because that will get rid of your ex-wife.'*
>
> *So, you do. So I had to go down and queue round the corner here. And that is a very sobering experience. Especially when you fill the form in and there's not enough gaps on the form to put your previous salary on.*
>
> *And it really does bring it home to you. That you are sat in a dole office on a Wednesday afternoon at 2.30 picking up your sixty odd quid a week. And it brings it home to you. Especially when you meet other staff in there."*

One suggested technique of dealing with this angle was to make appointments around that time. Go and have a coffee with a friend or an ex-colleague in order to make the trip a positive one. Then just quickly pop in and do what needs to be done and pop back and carry on chatting. Makes the whole process a little more invigorating for the soul.

Do more than one thing – it doesn't have to be one single thing that brings in the money. Subject to time constraints, you could look at a few different ventures which, together, earns you what you need.

Try not to work every hour that you can. You want to keep some time back for future planning.

Network marketing – there are a lot of MLM (Multi-level Marketing) companies around at the moment that enable you to build a decent income. There may be an upfront investment but not all of them are that high. If you get on well with people and are happy to promote products, could be a very good sideline to consider.

Look online – Don't ignore the possibilities of doing business online. Buying and selling products, even the providing of support services, are much more common online nowadays. If you're comfortable around computers, have a look into what other people are doing.

Go direct – if you're looking for paid employment, try knocking on a few company doors. Many businesses want to hire someone but can't afford to take on an agency. So by only looking at recruitment websites you miss out on a lot of opportunities. Go to a retail park, visit each company and ask if they are looking to hire.

Be an entrepreneur – get your thinking cap on. Take the Alan Sugar approach and just have a think about how to make money. What can you make cheaply and sell in the high street? Who needs their car washing or garden sorting out? What gets thrown away that might be of interest to someone else? Just go back to basics, watch some old episodes of the Apprentice and get creative.

> *"Basically I was sat on my arse at home thinking 'What the hell can I do?' So I had to invent myself after a period of doing nothing. So I said 'All I know is my old trade.' And that's where you need your friends to say, "Well. Think about it. If everybody's going through this crisis, what they need is that trade knowledge.'*
>
> *And then you have to invent yourself because then you think 'But nobody's going to take advice of me, are they? Because I've just gone bust.' and they say 'No. The opposite. You've just been through it. You're perfect to advise the bank or a client going down as to what happens.'*
>
> *And then it suddenly dawns on you, again because you're so negative, I didn't look at it from the right angle. How obvious!"*

No general CVs – this isn't a careers book, so I'm not going to tell you how to write a good CV etc. Just go onto Google and find some free tips. The key thing, however, is not to have one CV that you send out to everyone. See something you like and tailor your CV to that job. It takes longer, yes. But increases the likelihood of success.

Get the right mindset – If you go around thinking negative thoughts about how there aren't any jobs and you won't find anything, then congratulations! You get to be right. However, there are ways of making money out there and you just have to do a bit of searching before you find it. If not the first attempt, then the second. If not the second, then the third. And so on. And so on. It may take a while, but they are out there.

ACTION POINT 10.3 - Finding the ideal vocation

Right, you've got something in place that earns some cash or you have some time available before you need to take emergency action.

How do you work out what that thing is that you will enjoy doing and will fund the lifestyle you want?

As ever, there's no easy answer or formula. It will need you to be open minded, prepared to do some analysis and research and keep going over things until you get closer and closer to what it is you want.

The elements of a business

To start with you need to know what ingredients this ideal job or business has within it.

So start off with writing down what ingredients you will find in any money making enterprise. A good way of doing this is to work through a standard day at your old business. Or imagine a day in an imaginary career.

So, for example, the alarm would go at 7am. You'd get up and get dressed, check your emails on your iPhone then get into the car and drive half an hour to the office. Park outside, walk past the receptionist and get the lift up to your floor. Head into your office saying hello to your colleagues.

Okay, this might not be your day, but it isn't a ridiculous scenario. And the ingredients you can draw from this are:

- Hours of work
- Dress code
- Contact culture (i.e. are you contactable at all hours or are you strictly 9-5)
- Hardware support (phones, computers etc)
- Other benefits (e.g. company car)
- Geographical location

- Distance from house to office
- Transport options
- Parking facilities
- Working in an office
- Office facilities
- Location shared with other companies?
- Number of other employees
- Internal teams?
- Size of team?
- Office layout

The more you think about an actual job, the more ingredients will come out.

- Remuneration
- Frequency of payment
- Employment status
- Level of seniority

Also, think about skills that are used. Think about what you've actually done in the past and what has actually been involved. When we run our own businesses, it is surprising the things we end up doing. Far removed from our original idea.

- Managing
- Analysing numbers
- Writing reports
- Problem solving

Just add in as many things as you can think of. Over time you will add to this, so your first list will not be a complete one, but it's a good start.

Find some order

If you are writing all this down on paper, I suggest that now might be a good time to move to a computer and get a spreadsheet up and running. Nothing complicated, but it will help you move things around and add stuff in.

Redo the list in a rough order of importance. In basic terms, the most important element at the top (which might not be money, remember) down to the least important at the bottom. Precise ordering isn't important, just the general progression is needed.

One way is to just run down the list and give each number a score out of 10. That makes it quite easy to rearrange (and if on a spreadsheet, sorting becomes easy).

Find your range

Alongside each element, I want you to write down a

range within which you will be comfortable to work.

So, for remuneration it is quite easy. You've worked out your ideal figure already, just choose a range on either side of that that you feel would be acceptable.

Other things may be a bit harder to put in a range form, but it gets you thinking about what you like and don't like. It gets you thinking if you want to have your own business or work for someone else; what size company you might work for; if you're working with others and how many; amount of time on the road or outside; face to face time with customers; the level of social responsibility etc etc.

Some things may be a specific Yes or No.

By the end of this exercise you now have a rough blueprint of what your ideal job will contain. This will act as a filter going forward to help you think about what you can do that might be suitable.

Be observant

You will be continually revisiting and revising this list. Adding elements to it, rearranging the order of importance and fine tuning the range in which you are comfortable in working.

And you do this by looking at different jobs.

Anything and everything.

If you meet someone new, find out what they do. When you're watching the television and you see a newsreader or an actor or an actor playing a fireman, think about those jobs. Go back to previous jobs that you've done or jobs your parents did.

Go to free networking events and see who is on the attendance list. Go online and look at career websites and job postings or see who's posting on forums and chat rooms and what they do.

Every single job, career, pastime, vocation or form of paid activity is worth looking at in the name of research.

Because what you do for each one is think about doing that job.

What elements appeal?

What elements don't appeal?

And use them to calibrate your list.

Example

Maybe you're a Formula One fan and want to be Lewis Hamilton.

You like the elements where you get recognised for success, get to drive fast cars, get lots of money, be super fit.

But you don't like the media attention, the pressure

on you as an individual, the lack of a social life, the constant travelling and the risk of serious injury.

Compare it to your ingredients list. Not everything will be relevant, but see what changes it might make.

What can you add to the list? (Safe environment, for example).

Which items need to move around in terms of importance? (Social life may move up a notch).

Which range of figures do you need to adjust? (maybe happy to have a few other people around you).

This doesn't mean that you are going to become a Formula 1 driver, but you use it as a benchmark to test what is important to you.

Do the same for a newsreader, an actor, a fireman. Not with the intention of becoming them, but to draw out the elements that you really like and fine tune your ingredients list.

Devote time to it

I suggest that you reserve about an hour every day, or every other day depending on your circumstances, to work on your list. In between each session, find a way of noting down jobs that you spot that you will review in that time. Maybe carry a notebook around with you, or use the recording function on your smartphone to make a verbal reminder.

Once you get into the habit, your mind will become open to looking for new jobs and focussing on the differences and the similarities.

Eventually, you will be reviewing someone else's job and realise that it matches the majority of the top half of your list.

Now you're getting close to your ideal vocation.

It might not be perfect, but if you are a step closer, it is worth investigating and could be a possible stepping stone i.e. do that job and carry on exploring and fine tuning. As your ingredients are in a rough order, it helps you decide which ones you can sacrifice in order to achieve others.

But the closer the match to your ideal range, the more you are likely to enjoy it and the better you will be at doing it. In addition, the basic structure of your CV is already written, as you've already identified the areas that make you ideal for the role.

There's no set timescale to say how long this process will take, but once you get into the habit of doing it, even if you have to take an interim job just to get some cash in, you can still easily keep the process up.

But whatever you do, keep up with it and stop only when you are happy that the job you are doing is the job you want to do and gives you exactly what you want.

Summary

It is a cliché, but the world is your oyster.

If you fall into the propaganda trap of believing the media and the nay-sayers, then you may as well give up now.

But, there is something out there for you.

That may be doing what you've been doing. Never accept that the business is dead until you want it to be. The company may be gone but, if you believe that you can make money out of that trade, then there are ways of getting back into it.

If you want to do something completely different, now may be the ideal time to go and do just that. It may take a bit longer to find what you want, but it will be worth it once you do.

Then you can truly start to LET GO and move yourself towards a state of success.

CHAPTER 11 : SUMMARY AND CONCLUSIONS

I don't think I'm breaking any new ground when I say that 'Life is complicated'. When you combine the impact of the business curve and the personal curve, both of which have many different shapes and timings, it is virtually impossible to tackle every scenario.

I will, however, endeavour to try and summarise the main themes into five key areas which can be applied in pretty much any scenario.

1. Be really clear about what you want

Have a very clear image about what you, an individual, want from life. Which things are important, both materialistically and emotionally. Understand that where you are headed is the most important thing and what happens to you on the way is just stuff that happens. It may shape you, but it does not define you. When you know why you do what you do, you can choose the right battles to fight.

2. Separate the person from the business

Be aware that the two can exist independently, so don't confuse the performance of one with the other. Be clear about when you are wearing your business hat and when you are wearing your personal hat, especially when it comes to employees and major stakeholders such as the bank. Be aware that both elements need to be worked on and supported.

3. Raise your awareness levels

In terms of your business, make sure you know what the wider market is doing and be very clear about what measures you need to have in place to flag up early warning signs.

In terms of yourself, recognise your emotional behaviour. Try to understand what your behaviour might mean and think about how you can manage it. Be honest with yourself, otherwise how can you improve?

4. You can't do everything

Don't be afraid to ask for help. Be good at what you do, so give your brain time to relax so that you can stay on top form. Bring in experts to deal with the bits that you're not so good at.

There are always options available to you, you just might not be able to see them. Get into the habit of talking to others, even in the good times.

5. Act now

This is not a kid's game. There are no prizes for the

one that keeps quiet the longest. Even if it is the smallest of steps, such as talking to a friend or emailing a business contact, just get the ball rolling.

What's the worst that could happen if you did?

What's the worst that could happen if you didn't?

Changing a culture

There are two main conundrums that I, and many others, seek a solution for.

Firstly, how do you get people in difficulty to ask for help earlier?

Secondly, how do you ensure that, if the business does fail, the entrepreneur at the top gets back on their feet quickly.

Solving these issues will be a huge boost to our national economy. More successful businesses and fully active entrepreneurs can only be a good thing.

There is a common perception that the United States seem to have a better handle on the matter. The list of hugely successful individuals that have a string of business disasters behind them is much longer than in the UK.

Their ability to bounce back and move on appears to be much greater.

It is my personal opinion that this is purely a cultural thing and that there are two main elements where the States seem to approach things differently to the UK, that I think make a massive difference. Both have been touched on this book.

First of all, there is a big distinction between business failure and personal failure. Businesses are perceived as tools; as ventures. Things to try out. Some work and some don't and when they don't work, you move on and give something else a go.

The vision lies within the person, not within the corporation. So if you lose the latter it doesn't matter.

In the UK, when the business goes down, there is a much greater chance that it will drag the individual with it.

Secondly, American culture is much more open to asking for help.

There is a greater demand and acceptance over there for psychiatrists, coaches, mentors and so on. At any, and every, stage of life or business.

If we were in the habit of talking to people about our issues at every stage of our lives, then we would have no problem at all asking for help when things got really difficult.

Together, I think these two approaches to life make a huge impact. How you intentionally change a nation's culture is such a drastic way, I don't yet know.

Hopefully this book will help a few people to move in that direction.

A character building experience?

You will recall that this book came about because of a common phrase.

> *"It was one of the worst periods of my life...but I learnt so much as a result."*

Which led to me asking the question "So, what did you learn?"

Hopefully what you've grasped from this book is that, in general, they learnt about themselves. What they were made up of, what was important to them, how they interact with others and how they should react to different situations.

This led many of them to come up with a very similar phrase:

> *"I'm a better person for having gone through it."*

This then pushed me towards another question that I asked all of the contributors.

"Could you have become this better person without having to go through the pain of the insolvency?"

I am fascinated by this question. In part, I suspect, because I don't think it is possible to come up with a definitive answer. Whilst much will depend on the individual and how they react to situations in general, how can you genuinely test for the alternative scenario?

SUMMARY AND CONCLUSIONS

So, purely in the interest of philosophical debate, I include a representative sample of the various responses I received.

> *"I think you've got to say 'Yes'. Because otherwise I've got to go through something as traumatic as that to learn something, which I don't think is true ... that everybody has to go through a big major upheaval. Now some people just don't take that risk. They don't pioneer. Yeah, that's fine, okay. Maybe they take risks in other ways.*
>
> *So I think, yes, I could have become ... I mean I think life is about trying to become 'More' ... whatever that is. I think I could have tried to continue to become 'More' without going through that experience.*
>
> *So there's other people's experience and your experience, isn't there, in life. And if you were able to ... be close enough to somebody else's experience to think 'Hmm, I don't want to do that'. So ... whether there's a way to ... get close enough to somebody else's experience ... good or bad, and learn from it. Because if it's too much at a distance I don't think you're connected and you're not gonna take the lesson so well.*
>
> *I'm not sure. That's a really hard question to answer. How could I become more or a better*

person without having ... I'd just be a different kind of person, I suppose."

"I don't know if you can. I don't think you can, because you're constantly evolving and developing so you've got to have experiences to help you move. Otherwise you do just live in this pink fluffy cloud world and ... there's nothing wrong with failure really. Is there? As long as you know that where you're at now is ... you're better off as a result of it.

If you turn it into 'Well, how can I learn from it. What has it taught me?' And be honest with yourself. So that you don't repeat the same mistakes again."

> *"I think you do [have to go through it]. I think you do. I think it's really sad to say that you can't. How can you tell somebody who's 35, who's a multi-millionaire, not only on paper but is looking at Coutt's bank statements with well into 7 figures on deposit. Who gets phone calls from them saying "Mr W, you've got 80 grand in your current account. Do you want us to do something with it for you?' And every single month another 30 grand after tax hits your account.*
>
> *How do you tell that person, 'Do you think you should be more cautious with money?' It's really really hard. Or, you know, why don't you sell your business. You can't. I think it's incredibly difficult."*

"I think to truly, truly succeed you have to have failed ... at something. That's how I feel. Do you know what success is? Have you ever experienced failure to know what success is? But success isn't what ... people think success is driving a flash car. I had a flash car. I couldn't pay for it. I had a huge house and I couldn't afford to pay for it.

It's ... knowing that the bills are paid as well at the end of the month. Knowing that the VAT man can't come and knock on your door.

*But, as a person, I believe that to actually truly experience success you maybe have to have failed at something. The same goes in my marriage. I've had two failed marriages and I know that this one ... **I know** that it's successful. Because it feels like it is. I didn't have to have get married the other two times but ... I kind of know now. I'm not telling everyone to go out and get divorced, because I think that would be very wrong but er ... yeah."*

> *"If I could go back ... I'd go back ... If I could have structured it better, I'd have gone back ... to ... yeah, just after business had folded ... No, because I ... No!*
>
> *I'd have gone through it again!*
>
> *Yeah, because if I didn't know how hard it were, I probably could have built a business there and just crashed at the end, you know what I mean?*

And not been strong enough to pick myself back up again and go again.

Because if I didn't go down ... then I wouldn't have been feted to get up. Do you know what I mean? Personally, mentally and businesswise. So even though it were hell ... yeah I'd have gone in straight from the beginning again."

Overall, the general consensus appears to be pretty much 'No'. In order to become a better person, you have to experience the pain.

As mentioned, we will never know the truth for sure, however, you do have an interesting opportunity that these contributors never had.

You have an additional choice.

You can choose to take on board the learnings contained within this book and use them to avoid the hell that the others went through.

And that is a good thing.

Or you can choose to ignore the learnings. And, as the fire rains down in your own personal inferno, remember that you will make it through; that you will learn some amazing things about yourself; and you will become a better person for the process.

And that is also a good thing.

Two routes, both with a positive outcome. Which

one will you take?

The choice is yours.

LETTING GO - A final word from our contributors

> *"I have become quite big into the law of attraction. And I always wanted to make a lot of money. And it was clear that some of the people who are the proponents of the law of attraction say that you might end up in an entirely different sort of business that you hadn't thought about and I think that's what happened. And I think I'm set fair. In the next 10 years I can earn a lot of money.*
>
> *I've tackled a lot of stuff. I've faced a lot of demons. It was an interesting challenge but now I'm probably the most positive I've been in the last 10 years."*

"I don't mind now that I've experienced what you would traditionally label as failure. Fortunately, I didn't lose all my self-respect. I maintained my highest priority/job description which is being a dad. So I didn't lose everything in that sense.

But if I hadn't been through that loss I wouldn't be able to appreciate so much, I don't think. Somebody else came up with a phrase for it. It's kind of being 'Satisfied with what you've got whilst in pursuit of what you want' and I think I was perhaps previously somewhat dissatisfied with what I'd got whilst in pursuit of what I wanted.

Now, having been through, you know ... nothing ... I'm perfectly satisfied with what I've got. I feel more content, in that sense.

Beforehand, when I met my old mates from school and things like that, I sort of felt like I had to tell them about where I was heading and what it was gonna be like and 'Isn't that exciting?' Now, it doesn't matter to me at all, you know. So I'm probably a little less 'Ooh, look at me.'

So whilst I wouldn't wish the same circumstances on anybody, it isn't actually as bleak, or at least it hasn't been for me. I think it'll depend on individuals how they handle it as well. But the outcome hasn't been as bleak and isn't a total loss. There's been some good that's come out of if, there's been some values that I think are important that I hold dear that have come out of it. Like give and take in daily life and look for opportunities to help others, despite how busy you are. An appreciation of the present and the treasures that are in it, if you take the time to stop and look at them. The relationships that you have with people that matter to you are precious. They are worth investing some time in."

> "I've always seen light at the end of the tunnel. I've always seen there is a possibility, there is a way round something. You've just got to find it. There is a way round. Okay, so you owe somebody a bill. There is a way round it.

And things pass. Things always pass.

The only reason I can get past the dark times is I know it's going to pass. I know, I've just got to wait for that lowest point to arrive. I know it's terrible going through it at the time, but I do know there's always light at the end of the tunnel and I'm going to come out of if somewhere.

There's always something around the corner worth looking for. There's something that is enjoyable to look out for in life. Even if it's just a blade of grass to see or a smell of air. There is something in life to always look forward to.

Okay, you may not be in a situation where you want to be at this moment in time, but if you're careful and you work methodically through things, you'll get there."

"*I refer to it as negative, but then ... it's been a positive experience. It definitely feels negative at the time but ... I think as you develop as a person and become more realistic about how things work and, you know, what expectations are. Even though they are negative experiences, as long as you can gather them all up and use that failure to not repeat ... you know ... to somehow move yourself further along. Then they're negative in the moment but they've probably made you a better, more rounded person for that, really."*

> *"My cup's always half full. You know what I mean? I just know ... from, you know, just from life experience and from what I've taught myself, with all the positive attitude stuff and right/left brain and all that, that it's 95% attitude. If you've got the right attitude then you can overcome it and get something done about it."*

"Look at me. I did it and I'm still here. You're not going to die. You're still alive. What is the really worst thing that could happen to you. You could lose one of your parents, you could lose one of your kids. You haven't lost those. What you've lost is your business. That's what I would say to them.

It feels like the end of the world. But it's not. And it might feel like it for quite a while. But it really isn't. Think about what's the worst thing that could ever happen to you. What you could lose."

> *"Success is being happy. Success is getting up in the morning and enjoying what you're doing. It's not having twenty, thirty, forty grand in the bank. It's just being happy. All right, you need money to pay your mortgage.*
>
> *But success is being happy. Having a laugh. Enjoying life, that's success. Not driving about in a Porsche. Doesn't interest me that. And I think people with depression, if they get the materialistic things out of their head and just*

> *work on themselves, some way down the line those materialistic things will come, if they work on themselves, you know what I mean?*
>
> *It's gotta be you. You've got to be selfish about it when you're feeling shit or when you're going through that. It's gotta be me, me, me, me until you start feeling better. And then it can be you, you ... you know what I mean? Or us, us."*

*"I am the master of my own destiny. And bad things don't happen to you **because** it's you. You create your own success. What you do has an impact on what happens. Bad things don't always happen to you.*

I don't believe in being unlucky. You create your own luck, I believe that now.

And I'm very successful. I am a successful businesswoman now, even though I work for someone else. I'm also a really fantastic wife. I'm an awesome sister. And I'm a great daughter. And to me, those are the things that are important. And I'm a wonderful friend. And I think that if someone is my friend then I'd like to think that they're quite lucky.

But I'm skint.

And it used to be 'Oh I'm skint but ...'

But now it's, like, all those things 'Oh and by the way, I'm skint'.

Sounds silly, but I've got everything else I need. I'm not money driven at all. Although I still do like Dolce and Gabbana [laughs].

I'm in a fantastic place. I really am. I'm in the best place that I've been in my career. And I'm skint. But I'm in a really good place. Awesome place."

AFTERWORD

This has been a book based on the comments of others.

The comments expressed are the opinions of those that were interviewed and how they viewed their situation. Whilst I have tried to provide balance from any extreme views, either via other comments or my own experience, there will be some readers that hold a different opinion.

No matter how many people I interview, it will always represent a tiny percentage of the population that has experienced a corporate insolvency. I recognise, therefore, that the surface has only just been scratched.

I would hope, expect even, that there are further learning points to be gleaned.

Personally, I believe that it is possible to discover a bigger, better, more fulfilling life without having to go through such an emotionally traumatic episode. By sharing experiences and exploring a deeper understanding of what is truly important in life, I think we dramatically increase the chances of this happening.

Inspired by the people in this book, I have founded a community of business people who share the belief that there is more to business than just money.

Ultimately, we look to promote enjoyment as the key measure of success, not just sales and profit and work together to help each and every one of us to find that deeper sense of enjoyment in what we do.

Anyone that has been through an insolvency; suffered a near miss; or is a professional working in that arena, will have insights and experiences that will be of benefit to others. As we give, so do we receive.

Whilst the community is not specifically focussed on those facing insolvency, my hope is that someone facing their own difficulties will be able to get the support they need as part of that community.

The first step into the community is via regular meetings or free webinars called Breathing Spaces, that anyone one can get involved in. To find out more, either enter the following into your web browser:

www.businessenjoyment.com/breathingspaces

or go to the homepage of that website, click on **Community** and then select **Breathing Spaces**.

You will find more information there as to when the next meetings and webinars are being held and how to book on.

You have much to offer and I hope to see you there.

GLOSSARY

Here are some common terms that you may come across, either in this book or in your day to day dealings should things become difficult. They are relevant to legislation in England and Wales unless otherwise stated.

Many of the terms are complex legal matters and the explanations are stated in relatively simple terms in order to aid understanding. They can not be relied upon for legal purposes.

Administration

A formal *insolvency* process for companies. Appointment is very quick and is usually made by the company itself or by the *secured creditor*.

In very general terms, Administrations are used when there is still a business worth salvaging.

Administrator

An *IP* appointed to run the affairs of the company that has been placed into *Administration*.

ACCA

The Association of Chartered Certified Accountants. A global membership organisation of chartered accountants and one of the professional bodies that provides licenses to *IP*s in the UK.

Administrative Receivership

A formal *insolvency* process for companies. To the layman, very similar in appearance to an *Administration* except that appointment is only by a *Secured Creditor*.

Used to be the main insolvency process in England and Wales for many years until they were essentially replaced by *Administrations* in 2003.

Asset Finance

A form of lending backed by specific assets rather than cashflow. Most common form is the utilisation of debtors, such as *invoice discounting* and *factoring*. However, finance applied to stock, machinery and property is available.

Asset finance is often used in the purchase of businesses out of an insolvency process.

Bailiffs

Individuals who have been authorised to *distrain*, or seize goods from premises for non-payment of debt.

Most likely to be engaged by landlords and *HMRC*.

Bankruptcy

A formal *insolvency* process for individuals.

To clarify, in the UK, companies can not go *bankrupt*.

Big 4

The four largest accountancy practices in the UK all of which have substantial insolvency and restructuring divisions.

Namely: Deloitte, EY, KPMG and PwC.

CCJ

A County Court Judgment.

A court order made on a company or individual forcing it to make payment on an outstanding debt. If payment is still not forthcoming, it paves the way for the *creditor* in question to secure greater rights and powers, including the ability to appoint a *bailiff*.

Chapter 11

A formal *insolvency* process for companies in the United States of America. Very different to the UK.

Company Doctor

An experienced business advisor who will come into your business, review your processes and finances and then make recommendations on what you can do to turn things around.

Compulsory Liquidation

A formal *insolvency* process for companies arrived at as a result of the granting of a *Winding-up Order*. In the first instance, the *Official Receiver* will be appointed liquidator.

Usually applied to a company against their will, arising due to the non-payment of a debt, as opposed to a *Voluntary Liquidation*.

In general, means that the business can not be salvaged.

Creditor

A person or company who is owed money.

In an *insolvency*, there are three categories. *Secured*, *Preferential* and *Unsecured*.

CVA

A Company Voluntary Arrangement.

An *insolvent* company can enter into an agreement with its *creditors* to avoid formal *insolvency*. A proposal is put to *creditors*, often requiring them to take a reduction in their debt. The proposal requires over 75% of creditors voting to approve it.

A common process used for Football clubs as the company remains intact and it enables them to maintain their position within the league.

CVL

A Creditors Voluntary Liquidation.

A formal *insolvency* process for companies. Unlike a *Compulsory Liquidation*, the process is initiated by the directors and the appointment of the *Liquidator is* approved by *creditors*. The ultimate result is, however, not much different.

Debenture

A charge over a business often granted to a bank in return for funding. Not dissimilar to a mortgage over a house.

The existence of the debenture allows the bank to control the insolvency process.

Debtor

A person or company who owes money.

Distraint

The process by which debtor's goods are seized in lieu of non-payment of rent or taxes. Other types of *creditor* need court approval.

The distraining process is carried out by *bailiffs* who cannot force entry and have to carry it out during normal working hours.

Due Diligence

The investigation of a business prior to its purchase. Will involve a rigorous review of the financial situation and contracts to help determine the sale price.

During an *insolvency*, this process is severely restricted.

Factoring

A form of *asset finance*.

With factoring, the debtors are actually sold to a third party in order to raise immediate funds. Consequently, control and responsibility to collect lies with the funder.

Final Demand

Not actually a legal term and has no specific meaning. Is most commonly used by *creditors* chasing payment to indicate that they are running out of patience.

Fixed Charge

Security taken by a lender over a specific asset or assets.

Can relate to debts (in certain circumstances), property and some items of machinery.

The company that has granted the charge can not dispose of that asset without the permission of the *Secured Creditor*.

Fixed Charge Receivership

The appointment of a *Receiver* over a specific asset, as opposed to an entire business.

Most common usage is over property, known as an *LPA* appointment.

Floating Charge

Security taken over assets of a company that are more transient in nature, such as stock or the essence of the business itself and is the defining element of a *debenture*.

The company that has granted the charge can use these assets without having to refer to a *Secured Creditor*, unlike a *Fixed Charge*.

HMRC

HM Revenue & Customs.

A government body that deals with the inspection and collection of taxes such as PAYE and VAT.

IBR

Stands for Independent Business Review and is a report generated by a firm of accountants or business professionals with a view to evaluating the strength of a company along with recommendations as to next steps.

Is most frequently commissioned by banks enabling them to assess their strategy towards a client that is underperforming.

Consequently is often known as an Independent Bank Review.

ICAEW

The Institute of Chartered Accountants for England and Wales. A membership organisation of chartered accountants and one of the professional bodies that provides licenses to *IPs* in the UK.

IFT

The Institute for Turnaround.

A membership organisation dedicated to professionals working in the Restructuring and Turnaround community.

Insolvency

A formal process that deals with a company that is *insolvent*.

An individual, known as an *IP*, is appointed to take control of the company's assets and is tasked to maximise the realisation of those assets. The subsequent funds are then distributed to *creditors* in a specified order.

Insolvency Practitioner

An individual, licensed to advise on and undertake appointments in all formal insolvency processes, both corporate and personal.

The Insolvency Practitioner takes all appointments in a personal capacity. Whilst it is usual for an Insolvency Practitioner to belong to a larger organisation (frequently a firm of accountants or solicitors), the actual appointment is in the name of the individual.

Anyone who wishes to become an insolvency practitioner has to have sufficient experience and to pass the three JIEB examinations before a licence can be applied for.

Insolvent

A company is deemed to be insolvent if it, either:

a) has liabilities that exceeds assets; or

b) cannot pay debts as and when they fall due.

The point at which a company becomes insolvent is not always obvious and many companies can become insolvent without entering *insolvency*.

Invoice Discounting

A form of *asset finance*.

Similar to factoring, except that with invoice discounting, title and control of the debts remain with the company

IP

Common abbreviation for an *Insolvency Practitioner*

IPA

Insolvency Practitioners Association

A professional body whose purpose is to inform and regulate *Insolvency Practitioners*.

They also provide licenses to *IPs*.

JIEB

The Joint Insolvency Examination Board.

A body that sets the examinations essential to qualifying as an *Insolvency Practitioner*, one of the conditions needed before applying for a licence.

Liquidation

A formal *insolvency* process for companies.

In general, there are three types. *Compulsory Liquidation* and two types of *Voluntary Liquidation*:

CVL and *MVL*.

A Liquidation will result in the company being *Struck off* and usually means the loss of the business.

Liquidator

An *IP* appointed to liquidate the assets of an *insolvent* company.

LPA

Law of Property Act 1925. An unusually common piece of old legislation that is still used to appoint a receiver over a specific property.

Moratorium

A period of protection granted to a company preventing any legal action being taken against it.

Most frequently used in *Administrations* and in certain *CVAs*.

MVL

A Member's Voluntary Liquidation.

A formal process for winding up a company that is not insolvent. Hence the decision is made by the members of the company and the creditors will be paid in full.

Official Receiver

A government body appointed to deal with *Compulsory Liquidations* and *Bankruptcies*.

If there are no assets available in the estate to cover professional fees, it will remain with the Official Receiver. Otherwise they will pass the case over to an *IP*.

Phoenix Company

A company that has emerged from the collapse of another via the purchase of the business and assets out of *insolvency*.

A true phoenix company will be run by the same directors as the original company.

Preferential Creditor

A category of *creditor* that, in general, receives funds out of an *insolvency* ahead of *unsecured creditors* but behind *secured creditors*.

Preferential creditors are now limited to debts such as employee wages and pension deductions.

In the past, certain taxes, such as VAT, held preferential rights, but these have now been abolished and is no longer the case.

Pre-Pack

The process by which the business and assets of an *insolvent* company are sold immediately upon the appointment of an *insolvency practitioner* via some form of formal *insolvency* process.

The sales contract will be negotiated prior to appointment and, after appointment, it is the duty of the *insolvency practitioner* to explain to creditors why this approach was taken.

R3

The Association of Business Recovery Professionals is the leading organisation for *insolvency*, restructuring and turnaround specialists in the UK.

Receiver

An individual appointed by a *secured creditor* to take control, or 'receive', the assets of a debtor. A receiver normally has the power to sell the asset and distribute the funds to the secured creditor.

Secured Creditor

A category of *creditor* that, in general, is paid out of an *insolvency* ahead of other *creditors*.

In the majority of cases, this will be a bank or similar funder.

Statutory Demand

A legally recognised, formal request for an outstanding debt.

Where a Statutory Demand is ignored and there is no dispute, a *Winding-up Petition* may be applied for.

Struck Off

The removal of a company from the Company Register. This does not have to be as the result of an *insolvency*.

TMA

The Turnaround Management Association.

An international membership organisation dedicated to professionals working in the Restructuring and Turnaround community.

Turnaround Coach

A business coach dedicated to working with directors and business owners where the enterprise is in distress.

A business coach provides personal support in a work context.

Turnaround Director

A professional advisor that will be appointed as a Non-Executive Director of a company and actively advise and assist in the running of the business until it is on the road to recovery.

Unsecured Creditor

A category of *creditor* that, in general, receives funds out of an *insolvency* behind everyone else.

The average supplier will be an unsecured creditor.

Voluntary Arrangement

Any agreement between a debtor and creditors to avoid a formal insolvency.

There are two types of arrangement, one for companies, called a CVA and one for individuals, called an IVA.

Voluntary Liquidation

A formal *insolvency* process for companies.

In general, there are two types of *Voluntary Liquidation:* CVL and MVL.

A Liquidation will result in the company being *Struck off* and usually means the loss of the business.

Winding-up Petition

An application to court that a debtor company be put into *Compulsory Liquidation*. The petition will need to be heard in court before an *Winding-up Order* can be granted.

However, bank accounts will be frozen and the business likely to cease once a petition has been issued.

Winding-up Order

A court order following the hearing of a *Winding-up Petition*, placing the company into *Compulsory Liquidation* under the control of the *Official Receiver*.

Zombie Company

A company that is near the point of *insolvency* but just able to survive, neither failing nor thriving.

ABOUT THE AUTHOR

Andrew R Miller has over 16 years experience working in insolvency and turnaround for one of the Big 4 global accountancy firms, including a period spent in the insolvency unit of a well known high street bank. He is a qualified chartered accountant and passed the notoriously difficult Insolvency exams first time.

The nature of the work predominantly involved trading businesses that had gone into receivership or administration with a view to selling them as a going concern and saving the business and the employees.

Andrew has been involved in such diverse industries as bingo halls, shopping centres, furniture stores, cylinder manufacturers, timber mills, pet food and even oil rigs.

As Andrew progressed within the firm, he became more involved in internal management, which meant leading and motivating teams and helping individuals develop and better themselves. This, in turn, led to an interest in coaching.

In 2010, Andrew obtained the first of his two diplomas from The Coaching Academy and, in 2011, set up his own coaching business.

Andrew recognised the pressure that directors were under when their businesses ran into difficulties and how their ability to perform was severely hampered. This could lead to poor decision making, insufficient planning and frayed relations with professional advisors. This had nothing to do with their personal abilities, just a symptom of the incredible stress that they were under.

In addition, when a business did go bust, the director could be crushed by the process and it could take them one to two years to get back on their feet again.

As he got to know and work with more business owners at different stages of their business lifecycle, he discovered something quite remarkable. The vast majority of successful business owners weren't really enjoying themselves either.

Sure, they were doing something they liked to do, but surrounding that came stress, long hours, dissatisfaction, feelings of unworthiness and a general lack of purpose.

Naturally, an underperforming business will contribute to that stress, but the converse was not automatically true. A successful business does not guarantee a happy business owner.

More and more he was finding that what his clients were after, wasn't more sales and more money – but instead to feel happier, react to situations better and to enjoy life more.

Once you start looking into it you can find numerous examples of extremely rich, successful entrepreneurs suffering from intense stress and anxiety which can lead to, at best, a severe lack of confidence and at worst, depression and even suicide.

In other words, exactly the same outcome as if they'd lost their business.

This did not sound right and so, Andrew became very clear in his belief that if you're going to run your own business, then you should enjoy what you do. Otherwise, what's the point.

In 2017, he founded Business Enjoyment, dedicated to helping others find enjoyment in what they do and to promote enjoyment as the key measure of success, not just sales and profit.

Naturally, making money is an essential ingredient, and ongoing support for business owners in difficulties is fundamental, but there is so much more to it than that.

If you want to find out more, go to

www.businessenjoyment.com

and see how you can get involved.

OTHER BOOKS BY ANDREW R MILLER

MORE THAN JUST MONEY
An Introduction To The Business Enjoyment Model *(due early 2019)*

MLM REVISITED
Fall Back In Love With Your Network Marketing Business *(due late 2018)*

MULTIPLY YOUR SUCCESS
The Business Owner's Workbook For Wealth And Opportunity

THE SUCCESSFUL BUSINESS OWNER'S GUIDE TO REDUCING STRESS
How to Avoid These 13 Common Pitfalls

SUCCESSFUL START-UPS
Get Going. Stay Going

All available on Amazon

or at

www.bit.ly/enjoybooks

where you will find more information on each book, along with access to the audio and video versions of The Successful Business Owner's Guide to Reducing Stress.

Printed in Great Britain
by Amazon